How to Pee Standing Up

Tips for Hip Chicks

BY ANNA SKINNER

ILLUSTRATIONS BY SARA SCHWARTZ

doWn tOwn press

New York London Toronto Sydney

 DOWNTOWN PRESS, published by Pocket Books
1230 Avenue of the Americas
New York, NY 10020

Copyright © 2003 by 17th Street Productions, an Alloy Company
Illustrations copyright © 2001 by Sara Schwartz/http://saraschwartz.com

This edition specially printed for Barnes & Noble Books by Simon & Schuster, Inc.

First Downtown Press hardcover edition February 2007

10 9 8 7 6 5 4 3 2

DOWNTOWN PRESS and colophon are
trademarks of Simon & Schuster, Inc.

Manufactured in the United States of America

ISBN-13: 978-1-4165-3817-2
ISBN-10:   1-4165-3817-8

For information regarding special discounts for bulk purchases,
please contact Simon & Schuster Special Sales at 1-800-456-6798
or business@simonandschuster.com.

How to Pee Standing Up *isn't just about liberating yourself from skanky toilet seats. Nope. This little book aims higher than that. (Pardon the pun!) The survival tips you're about to read will teach you the kind of skills you need to be a "kick ass and take names" kind of female—tackling life's missions with attitude and finesse. So for those of you who want to be sneaky, not saintly; who kick butt, not kiss it (unless, of course, kissing it gets you one step up the ladder); who delight in being bad and doing good; and who always think of yourselves, please read on. And feel free to add a few tips of your own.*

TABLE OF CONTENTS

1. BEAT THE BANK
How to get out of debt without having to get out of town . . . page 7

2. BLUE-CHIP BABE
Tips for living large on a salary that isn't . . . page 11

3. BOSS FROM HELL
Tips on handling the most heinous of honchos . . . page 17

4. BREAKUP
How to dump with your dignity intact—and most of your good CDs . . . page 25

5. DIAL-UP
Chatting long-distance for the low, low price of free . . . page 31

6. DITCH THE DATE
How to break a bad date without breaking any hearts . . . page 35

7. EVIL LANDLORD
How to get what you need when your shower is cold, your apartment is hot, and the roaches are plotting a takeover . . . page 41

8. FIRST CLASS
Scamming your way to the free champagne, or at least saving enough cash to afford drinks in coach . . . page 47

9. FRIENDSHIP FIXES
Can't live with 'em, can't whack 'em upside the head: how to ease out of a friendship that's past its prime and fix one that you've dirty-dogged . . . page 51

10. FRONT ROW
How to score the Sweet Seats without selling an organ . . . page 55

11. GREASE THE PALM
Learn the subtle art of persuasive payola . . . page 59

12. GROOVEABLE FEAST
How to get down without getting arrested . . . page 63

13. HIGHWAY TO HELL
How to stay on the right side of Officer Big Stick . . . page 69

14. HIT THE ROAD
Rev up for a road trip, an exotic getaway, or a break for the border . . . page 75

15. HOME FOR THE HOLIDAYS
How to navigate the rocky terrain of family events without getting disowned . . . page 81

16. HOME REMEDY
Easy outs for embarrassing ailments . . . page 85

17. J.O.B. BLUES
How to land a kick-ass job and survive the ones that suck . . . page 93

18. KICK ASS
Self-Defense 101 . . . *page 97*

19. LADY LUCK
If you're going to win more than free drinks, you have to know how to play the game . . . *page 101*

20. LET'S MAKE A DEAL
Nine savvy tips for your next negotiation . . . *page 107*

21 MOBILIZATION
Car Repairs 101 . . . *page 113*

22. MORNING AFTER
Taming the hangover heaves after a night of too much fabulousness . . . *page 119*

23. PEE STANDING UP
How to answer nature's call anywhere, anytime . . . *page 123*

24. PINK SLIP
How to get—or give—the ax with maximum style. Extra points for poise; extra-extra points for unemployment checks . . . *page 127*

25. SCAM CITY
Front rows, free food, and the hottest fashion: our favorite hustles that will make them yours for the taking . . . *page 131*

26. SCHMOOZING, SOCIALIZING, AND SURVIVING THE SPOTLIGHT
How to make friends, influence people, and address a crowd without losing your lunch . . . *page 135*

27. STYLE PILE MAKEOVER
Redecorate your swankienda on a dime . . . *page 139*

28. SWEET REVENGE
How to revel in the joys of payback while staying on this side of psycho . . . *page 145*

29. TABLE FOR TWO
Get past the bitchiest maître d' without promising your first-born . . . *page 149*

30. UNDERCOVER
The right getup for every setting, from Meet the Parents to Lunch with Your Ex . . . *page 153*

31. VELVET ROPE
How to get past the Door Guy when you're not a super-model, a celeb, or a sultan's girlfriend . . . *page 157*

BEAT THE BANK

mission:
To pull yourself out of the red and into the black.
(And who doesn't look great in black?)

So there you are, swinging through life buying a teensy bauble here, an itty-bitty new purse there, and occasionally taking that hottie down the hall to a nice little din-din to cheer him up after a lousy audition. "Everyone deserves a little pampering now and then," you tell yourself. Your friends tell you the same thing, sympathetically—especially when you're picking up the check. And that's when you get the call. You know the one—it's usually from a Mr. Green or a Ms. White, and it almost always begins with something misleadingly polite like, "We'd like to speak to you right away about your credit card balance." "Why are they bothering me?" you ask. "It was just a pair of shoes!" you think. And finally: "What's with the color-coded pseudonyms?"

We hate to inform you, but you've fallen into the dreaded Deadly Debt Trap. All credit cards should come with a label: Warning! Warning! Credit cards are not free money! But they don't, and before you know it, you're maxed out and have zero money left over after paying your bills. How's a person supposed to lead a fabulous life with a budget of nada?

Stupid Reasons for Going into Credit Card Debt

1. Gucci brings out my green eyes.
2. With a big-screen TV like that, who needs a boyfriend?
3. My honey may be a deadbeat, but he's my little deadbeat!
4. Bloomingdale's is on my way to work. Like that's my fault.
5. By buying those Ralph Lauren sheets on sale, I'm actually saving money!

Having credit card debt is like wearing a heavy ankle bracelet (we're talking house arrest, not a fashion accessory) 24/7. It keeps you from building any kind of savings, including your See Ya Sucker Stash (see Hit the Road), and can make it harder for you to rent apartments, get loans, or buy a house.

Proper Credit Card Conduct

1. Transfer your balances to cards that earn you freebies, like airline mileage.
2. Transfer your balances to a card that has an extremely low APR* (like no interest for a year), then try to pay it off before that introductory APR is raised.
3. Always pay more than the minimum, but not so much that you don't have enough to pay other bills.
4. Finally, screen your calls—no need to let "Mr. White" ruin your night. Just be sure to pay the bill the next day.

Tips for Getting out of Debt

1. Don't live in denial. Figure out everything and everybody you owe.

2. Lower your expenses. Tap into your inner Disciplinarian, who can slap down your inner Princess from time to time. When you start to whip out the plastic, ask yourself: "Oh, fabulous one, is this a need or an indulgence?" Learn to tell the difference between the two; indulge when you have the cash in hand, but try to do it cheaply. (See Blue-Chip Babes.)

3. Increase your income. Get two jobs (it can be done) or a higher-paying gig until your debt is paid off.

4. Get help. Call the Consumer Credit Counseling Services at (800) 577-2227.

*APR: Aaah, a term we've all grown to know and love. It stands for **Annual Percentage Rate**—in other words, the cost of not paying off that balance. Hey, those credit card folks don't phone because they want to hear how your day went.

BLUE-CHIP BABE

mission:

To please your inner Rich Bitch without taking down a liquor store.

A bad salary is worse than a rotten mission: A mission has a beginning and an end, but having a busted bank account can make you feel trapped. It can also send you into Debtor Hell, running up Visa accounts willy-nilly in an attempt to live large on a paycheck that isn't. Fact: Going into debt is never glamorous.

But it just isn't easy maintaining one's wicked ways on a budget that's more Bud and beans than cocktails and caviar. For those of you who know that true style is measured by how much your feet hurt, here are a few savvy tips.

Style

Without glamour, we may as well be Jane Doe. And let's face it, Miss Jane is a dull girl.

1. Offer to model for a hair salon (preferably one that doesn't have Super in its name), in exchange for free haircuts and highlights.

2. For cheap style ideas, cruise used bookstores for cool '50s and '60s cookbooks (for entertaining ideas) and '70s fashion and decor books (for funky style).

3. Carry your bad self into any high-end boutique or department store and try on the most expensive thing. If you lose your nerve, just pretend you're Courtney Love, the high priestess of brazenness. If you're really good, the sales staff will have no idea that you have exactly $19 in your checking account. This is also an excellent exercise in role playing.

4. Invest in two bottles of nail polish—I recommend Cherry Red for when you're feeling nice and Blood Red for naughtier times—nail polish remover, and a nail file. Give yourself weekly manicures and pedicures, changing colors to suit your mood. This will make you feel high-maintenance.

5. Buy a car that's vintage and stylish (like an old El Camino); this way, it will appear that your crappy car is really an aesthetic choice.

Bathe Like a Goddess

Combine two cups of fine sea salt (at your grocery or health food store) with one ounce of oil (grapeseed, sweet almond, or olive) and six to eight drops of pure, essential oil (rose or lavender is nice). Mix well. Gently massage the salt all over your naked bod (excluding the face and neck), picking up what falls into the tub and reusing it. Then fill your tub with water.

Shelter

Your shelter is the sanctuary in which you'll recover from the oh-so-draining pressure of a fabulous life on the go. These are small touches that can turn your modest little hovel into a full-on swankienda.

1. Always keep a bottle of champagne in your refrigerator, and be sure to toast yourself in the tub (hey, just for being you!) while you watch your toenails dry.

2. Keep a few extravagant food items in your refrigerator—like $12 brandied peaches from France or perishable Hawaiian honey. You don't have to open them; it's enough to know that they are there.

3. Subscribe to high-style "shelter" magazines instead of buying them on the stands (where 3 issues cost the same price as a year's subscription). You'll find excellent ideas about how the jet set decorate their villas, castles, and, well, jets.

4. Imbibe at home (preferably not alone) and only high-end liquors. You can make Sapphire (a color that looks great on everyone) martinis at home for less than $2 a tipple.

5. Find a male submissive in the personal columns, and order him to come clean your house.

Trade in your unwanted CDs (here's a tip: anything from your boy-band days) for new ones (such as the rockin' sounds of hipper boy-band The Strokes or the sexy grooves of Zero 7) at used record stores.

Some Extravagant delicacies

Blue-Chip Babe Tip #2

Drop into a swank gym, and tell them you're interested in signing up but would like to try out the facilities first. Then have your very own day at the spa—and never go back. Hey, it's legal!

Stepping Out

The social arena is a good place to test your disguises—with or without the troops.

1. Taxi! If you are carless, occasionally splurge on cab rides instead of schlepping it on the bus. You'll feel important, even if your destination is the dump where you flip burgers.

2. Here's a handy disguise with unlimited benefits (including discounts all over your town): the poverty-stricken student. Snag a student ID from a junior or city college by signing up for classes. Even if you drop out, you can keep the ID (and all of its perks).

3. Buy cheap-seat balcony tickets to the opera, ballet, symphony, or musicals (but only if it's *Cabaret*), and sneak down to the empty seats in the orchestra section during intermission. (For Advanced Operatives: Visit the Founders Room, where all the high rollers hang out, and act as if you belong there.*)

* Extra points if you score free drinks.

4. Take yourself to high tea at the swankiest restaurant or hotel in town once a month. It won't cost that much, and you'll feel like the glamorista you really are.

5. Visit art openings at trendy galleries for free wine and elbow-rubbing with the arty types and wanna-bes. The art world has many subjects to study, especially if you're interested in the type who "longs to belong" but has no observable talent other than the gift of gab. (For Advanced Operatives: Scam your way into an after-opening dinner or party.)

Another option: Get a job that gets you access. If you work for a magazine or a record company, you'll get invited to lots of parties and score freebies that will help offset the lousy pay.

Personal Shopper, Please

If you're not into used closing stores and bargain bins, learn to consolidate your wardrobe purchases into two yearly outings. Save toward that preset date, and then use your budget to buy a few fashion essentials. Here's a little-known fact: Many clothing stores offer the services of a personal shopper—even the chains like Banana Republic. Call ahead and make an appointment. Once there, explain your needs—conservative job wear or funky fashion—and be firm about the amount you have to spend. Then your P.S. can recommend the three or four "must-haves" for the season and your wardrobe. It's a sensible way to stay up-to-date and keeps you from getting nickeled and dimed throughout the year on low-quality stuff you'll wear once and never use again.

Skip the Meals Out

Perhaps the most important words in the vocabulary of a Blue-Chip Babe on a Budget are "No thanks. I ate earlier." Here's the deal: Drinks and fun = necessities of life. Twenty-five-dollar chicken plate = extravagance. There's no reason why you can't join everyone for the party after dinner. (Hey, that's when the fun really begins anyway.) So learn to feed yourself at home, then join your friends later.

> *Blue-Chip Babe Tip #3*
> Find a fancy hotel and sneak a swim in its heated pool. Note: This is equally satisfying if done alone or with another Operative. Ultrasatisfying if done with a very buff operative.

BOSS FROM HELL

mission:

To survive the workplace when the head honcho is a creep.
Extra points for getting him or her fired.

Let's face it—a rotten boss can be one of life's biggest drags. Having such a boss means you will be faced with someone you find repellent on a daily basis, often before you've had any coffee. Worse, you will be forced to be civil to this person, even smile at this person, and generally avoid throwing anything heavy in his or her direction. For an employee who's used to expressing her opinion, occasionally by throwing things, this situation can quickly become torturous.

After considerable experience with the dreaded Boss from Hell, we have found that they fall into one of four categories—the Moron, the Power Perv, the Passive-Aggressive, and the Bully—with frequent crossovers occurring. *Note: If you find yourself facing a boss who is a combination of all the aforementioned categories, you should regard the situation as hopeless. Find yourself a good headhunter, and get the hell out of there.*

The following characteristics indicate the presence of an official Boss from Hell.

You know you're dealing with a Boss from Hell when he or she:

* Reams you for coming in five minutes late, then calls you "Baby Cakes" five minutes later.
* Asks you to brainstorm some ideas, but stares silently at you when you do.
* Steals your ideas without giving you credit.
* Takes too much of a creepy interest in your personal life.
* Hires you, then doesn't speak to you again for the next three months.
* Only notices your mistakes, and likes to mention them loudly in the break room.
* Throws tantrums with no provocation.
* Throws tantrums with provocation.
* Sets you up to take the fall.
* Doesn't describe what is expected of you and then yells when you don't "do your job."
* Asks you to cover while he or she plays hooky.
* "Forgets" to pay you overtime.
* Guilt-trips you for taking maternity leave.
* Chases you around the desk—or anything else—in the office.
* Asks you to do a cocaine run.

The Moron

By moron, we mean the kind of boss who says astonishingly stupid things with equally astonishing frequency. This is the mildest type of Bad Boss, but that doesn't mean he or she won't drive you bananas. Instead of stressing about it, write down the stupidest comments, and tell yourself you'll write a book one day. Also, take comfort in the fact that you will clearly take this boss's job in a matter of months, if not days.

THE POWER PERV

How bad can these bosses be? The following tragic story is true. The names have not been changed, in the hopes that the employee whose story it is may reap maximum vengeance.

"My mission began when Burt, a wealthy German financial planner, decided to get in the movie biz and hired me as his production assistant. My duties, in addition to typing his memos, were to prepare his morning drink of green tea made from twigs. Since I didn't like fetching drinks for people who signed my paychecks, I'd space out and sometimes boil his tea for too long. He would get worked up and accuse me of trying to kill him; it wasn't long before I started doing it on purpose *[an oldie-but-goodie passive-aggressive Double-Agent trick]*. Burt's favorite thing to do, besides bitch about his tea, was to talk about sex. He was married to a hippie chick thirty years his junior, and he claimed they had an 'open marriage.' *[Note: This term, coming from a boss, should be taken as a red flag.]*

"Burt began to insist that I eat lunch with him at his favorite Thai place. He'd sit and talk about his experiences in Thai brothels, boasting that he always had two girls *[puh-leaze!]*. It wasn't long after that when he began to stare at my breasts and slowly invade my personal space while talking to me. I would have quit, but I needed the money and didn't have another job lined up. One day, old Burt finally snapped and began chasing me around the office—*[a clichéd but not uncommon sitch]*. Finally, when I was trapped between him and my desk, I raised my hand, warning him to stop. The next thing I knew, the creep grabbed my pinky finger and bent it back. This was clearly a weird seduction move—even for lechy Burt—to say nothing of the fact that it hurt like hell. That was it for me: I slugged him in the bicep. *[See Self-Defense.]* Burt grabbed his arm and slithered back to his office. After that, he laid off for about a month. And by the time he started leering at me again, I had already given notice."

—as told by a happily self-employed Operative

Five Ways to Stop the Power Perv

1. Tell the P.P. to cut it out. Simple but surprisingly effective, this move is important because Pervs are capable of reading a come-on into every comment, no matter how benign. (You say, "Can you hand me my coffee cup?" He hears, "Would you find a way to brush your hand against my chest?") So be direct: "This is making me uncomfortable, and I want to keep the door open." That's hard to misinterpret, even for a Power Perv.

2. Document, document, document. If Step #1 doesn't work, you'll need backup for the eventual complaint.

3. File a complaint with your Human Resources department. If he still can't keep his hands to himself, go to a supervisor and give him up.

4. Punch the Power Perv. *Note: Only recommended for hand-to-hand combat situations similar to previous page. Otherwise, you'll just have to fantasize about it.*

5. File a harassment suit. With your settlement, fly to Costa Rica and write that tell-all novel, exacting maximum revenge.

THE PASSIVE-AGGRESSIVE

Passive-Aggressive bosses don't tell you what you need to know to do your job successfully. Ever fearful of confrontation, the P.A. will never criticize you to your face, but she or he *will* talk trash behind your back.

Remember the 3 F's when dealing with classic Passive-Aggressive foes:

1. Flattery

When in doubt, flatter (one of our favorites). If the P.A. is female, she'll feel like you recognize her innate fabulousness. If the P.A. is male, well, ditto.

> Sample Comment: "My favorite part of the presentation was that hilarious accounting anecdote you told at the end. How did you ever come up with it?"

2. Forge Ahead

If he or she is procrastinating in giving you the info you need to complete a project, see the job through to completion on your own and deal with the fallout later. *Note: Feel free to play the Flattery card here, too.*

Extra points for combination of **Forging and **Flattery.***

> Sample Comment: "I went ahead and called Steve for those numbers. I laid them out the same way you did in your last report—I thought it was much more clear."*

3. Facts

Always keep your boss posted in writing (memos, e-mail) of everything you're working on. And when she pisses you off, which she undoubtedly will, don't fly off the handle. Instead, calmly discuss the facts.

> Sample Comment: "I'm sorry you're surprised that I turned the report in before you had a chance to see it. If you'll check your e-mails and the note I left on your desk, you'll see I did let you know that I was working on it and that I would turn it in on Monday."

THE BULLY

This type of boss is the most easily identified of the four types—usually by how often he or she throws desk objects or coffee mugs across the room.

Bully Bosses come in many shapes and sizes—screamers and threateners, male and female. Similarly, the Bully is not discriminating when it comes to choosing a victim. But you can bet that if you are popular, competent, or given to high moral standards and solid integrity, you will be a prime target. The Bully Boss will see you as a potential threat and attack with a vengeance (and in the worst cases, with a stapler). What triggers an outburst? Sticking up for someone who's being victimized in the office, challenging the status quo, or—most dangerously—showing the potential to expose your boss's lousy job performance.

Since Bully Bosses are usually completely incapable of normal social interaction, they rely on their formidable skills of deception. B.B.'s generally don't have real talent; they've found other ways to make it to Boss-dom. That's why they are usually adept at lying and at escaping accountability for their actions. Combine these characteristics with their habits of dispensing relentless criticism, undermining comments, ridiculous workloads, and unrealistic deadlines, and it's enough to break even the toughest employee.

Steps You Can Take to Counter the Bully Boss

1. Write down every instance of bullying and keep it private. (Operative Lesson 101: Do not leave this valuable information on the hard drive of your computer at work.)

2. Save any bullying correspondence (e-mails, memos, etc.). When the Bully makes yet another idiotic accusation, ask for evidence supporting his stupid claim and even ask him to put it in writing. He'll probably back down like the coward he is, but if he keeps it up, let him know—again, in writing—that making unsubstantiated allegations is a form of harassment.

3. If he forces it, go the Tattletale route. Talk to personnel and file a complaint. Try to stay away from personal or

opinionated complaints. ("She's a cretin and has a cheap haircut" won't get you anywhere.) Instead, coolly concentrate on the Bully Boss's actions, and show them the evidence. Note: Human Resources usually sides with upper management as long as the department is performing well. Also, don't forget: Bullies are exceptional liars.

4. If Step #3 fails, call in the Mouthpiece. Talk to a lawyer.
5. Of course, if you've gotten to Step #4, you'll probably be on your way out. At some point, a wise girl knows when to move on.

Boss from Hell Fact:
Bully Bosses rarely change. When you quit, they will find a new target.

BREAKUP

mission:
**To survive a breakup with your mind, body, and spirit intact—
and without losing any of your good CDs.**

Breakups can be dangerous terrain. A bad breakup (usually
the kind where you're the Breakup-ee) can make you feel puny (and occasionally vengeful—see Revenge); a good one (usually the kind where
you're the Breakup-er) can be one big sigh of relief.

A really bad breakup story:

Once upon a time, there was a girl in love (let's call her Jane
Schmo), whose boyfriend suggested they get his-and-hers tattoos.
At the tattoo parlor, her boyfriend (we'll call him Dick Little) insisted
she go first. So Jane gritted her teeth while Dick's name was etched
onto her backside. When the tattoo was finished, Dick checked it
out to make sure his name was spelled right (how many ways can
you spell Dick?), then announced that he was dumping Jane and
walked out of the tattoo parlor and Jane's life for good.

The moral of this story? Don't date a Dick!

Sorry—another way to look at it is that if a guy dumps you, he's not worth your time and certainly not worthy of you, so just be thankful you didn't tattoo his name on your ass.

Here's a question: Is it worse to be the Dumper or the Dumpee? Sure it hurts to get the heave-ho, but sometimes it's even crappier to be the one doing the heaving. Your ego isn't as banged up, but you're left with all the responsibility (and guilt). Here are some basic strategies to manage your way through both ends of a Big Breakup.

(ditch memories)

DUMPER DON'TS:

1. Don't take on the dreaded guilt trip! Staying with someone out of pity is gross, not to mention downright selfish. Think of it this way: You're cheating your would-be ex—and yourself—out of moving on to the Next Great Thing. You may think you're doing someone a favor by sticking around beyond the Bitter End, but let's face it: That last queasy month or two will only bring sour feelings and a couple of episodes of really bad sex. Wake-up call: Change is the only constant in life. Move on.

2. Don't draw it out by having looong talks with the Dumpee about what went wrong, whose fault it was, why you've changed, blah, blah, blah. It makes us tired just writing about those conversations. (Can you picture Foxy Brown doing that relationship rap? We

Dating After a Breakup
Spit out that bitter pill. Keep your heart open when you start to date again. Don't hold the sins of the ex against a potential new hottie.

Breakup Tip #1

Sometimes it's easier to take the blame for breaking up a relationship than it is to try to explain why your boyfriend's ear hair really bugs you. On the other hand, this method is not appropriate if the significant other has done something really heinous. In that case, you are free to tell him exactly why you'd rather be sentenced to wear culottes and clogs for the rest of your life than spend another minute as his main squeeze.

didn't think so.) Here's the deal: Be nice (remind your Dumpee of what makes him or her so great), but be firm about your intentions (and the clear steps you're ready to take—i.e., giving him a deadline for moving out). And never let the talk degenerate into a blame game.

3. Don't try to stay friends. This is a classic trap we've all fallen into, so read this closely: Instead of making your ex feel "safe" by sticking around, you are making him or her feel like crap. Cut the ties that bind.

4. Don't recycle. Too many of us end up repeating the same relationship missteps over and over again. In other words, think long and hard about what it was that turned you off about your ex. The reasons could be deep (he's selfish) or, let's face it, shallow (he wears acid-washed jeans). Either way, learn to avoid Mr. Selfish Acid-Wash Guy (or whatever your peculiar little weakness is) in the next go-round.

DUMPEE DO'S:

1. Do break off all contact. The Setup: You tell yourself that you just want to talk to him, that it's easier if you "stay friends." The Fall: There you are, having a beer somewhere as "friends," when suddenly you bust out crying right into your pale ale and embarrass you both by asking to have his baby. Instead of humiliating yourself, box all those pictures of you and "Honey" (and anything else that's a reminder) and throw them

in the back of your closet until you get hold of your tender self.

2. Do wallow in self-pity. Hey—it's good for you! By letting yourself feel miserable, you're helping the healing process along. So download a Patsy Cline box set, and get real down-and-dirty pitiful, if only for the night.

Breakup Tip #2
Never drink and dial. Here's a guarantee: The moment your ex picks up the phone, you'll feel like a total loser—especially when he or she hangs up on you.

3. Do pamper yourself silly. Here's a to-do list of doctor-recommended therapies for the recently dumped:

   * Get a massage.
   * Buy self flowers.
   * Purchase wildly sexy top/shoes/lingerie and revel in your sensuality. (You're still sexy even though you're partner-free!)
   * Listen to righteous-type music.
   * Convene best friends for revenge-fantasy session.
   * Treat self to vacation, or if broke, treat self to movie filmed in preferred vacation setting.
   * Hug pet; swear to pet it will be most important partner from now on.
   * Eat recklessly unhealthy foods.
   * Keep nails painted in I-Will-Survive-and-Conquer red.
   * Revel in shamelessly luxurious hot baths.

4. Do reconnect with yourself. Shift your perspective from "I just got dumped" to "What the hell did I learn from this (besides 'never date a man prettier than me')?" Take long hikes, see a therapist, try something new (knitting, painting, acting, karate).

5. Do rebound, rebound, rebound. **There's nothing like a little fling to boost that ego after a dumping. Sometimes the gods drop little surprises into your lap right when you need them most. Just make sure it's a no-harm rebound, meaning not with your ex's brother, father, or best friend.**

Big, Bad Breakup No-No's

You know you're handling your breakup poorly if any of the following happens:
· Your ex calls the cops and/or obtains a restraining order.
· You set anything on fire.
· You tap into your ex's voice mail or e-mail (although this move is slightly admirable for demonstrating surveillance skills).
You know who you are. Calm down and get some help.

The Yo-Yo:
This form of ex is the most destructive of all. He convinces you that he can't exist without you (it's the poetry that always sucks you in, am I right?), then forgets your next two dates. Avoid this one like the plague—he'll wipe out your self-esteem faster than you can say, "I'll have a gallon of Cherry Garcia in a cup, please."

DIAL-UP

mission:

**To bilk the phone company out of your
long-distance nickel. Better yet, it's legal!**

There's nothing a savvy girl loves more than getting something
for nothing. Especially if that something involves chatting with friends in
exotic places like Monaco, Mozambique, and Toledo. And if you're already
paying for an Internet connection, you'll be happy to know that you never
have to pay for another long-distance call again. Listen up: Getting free
long distance is almost as good as getting free shoes. Almost.

The Deal:

They call it Internet telephony (but you can call it Internet long distance),
and it works something like this: If you have a computer and an Internet connection (like Earthlink or AOL), you can go to an Internet LD site (see The
Sites to See in this chapter), download their software, and talk to your
compadre in Kansas for free, even if you live in Hawaii. (We wish we were
in Hawaii. We love Hawaii.) Connections can be made from PC to PC

(provided your callee has the right software) or PC to phone, depending on the vendor you use. *Note: Telephony setups are geared mainly to PCs right now, but there are a few vendors that offer programs for Macs.*

Dial-Up Tip #1

For the clearest sound, get a high-quality headset with a built-in microphone. *Note: High-quality doesn't necessarily mean the most expensive. Shop around and compare.*

The Catch:

There always is one, isn't there? Internet long distance still has some kinks. Potential problems: poor sound quality and/or a bad connection. So while telephony may be ideal for chats with friends and good old Aunt Myrna (where sometimes a poor connection can be a good thing), we don't recommend it for business calls. Shop around: If one program doesn't work for you, try another.

Dial-Up Tip #2

The faster your modem speed, the better. Make sure yours is at least 56 kbps. If you have a cable or DSL connection, you're in great shape.

Dial-Up Tip #3

Make sure your sound card is full-duplex. You can use the microphone and speakers that come with it, but you're better off with the headset, which can block out external noise.

The Sites to See

Internet long-distance vendors are like many other Web sites; often here today and gone tomorrow. Listed below are available vendors as of this printing.

- iConnectHere *(http://www.iconnecthere.com)*
- Dialpad *(http://www.dialpad.com)*
- HotTelephone.com *(http://www.hottelephone.com)*
- MediaRing *(http://www.mediaring.com/index.phtml)*
- Net2Phone *(http://www.net2phone.com)*
- PhoneFree.com *(http://www.phonefree.com)*
- BuddyPhone *(http://www.buddyphone.com)*
- CallServe—for Europe *(http://www.callserve.com/langselect.asp)*

Not all of these sites offer free programs. But if you have to pay, it'll be a small amount (a penny a minute, as opposed to 5 to 7 cents a minute, which is what most telephone companies charge).

DITCH THE DATE

mission:

**To identify a lame date before it even starts;
to escape one with maximum flair.**

First Step: Identification
TYPES OF BAD DATES

After careful (and frequently painful) studies, we've found that most bad dates fall into one of a few distinct categories.

CLASSIFICATION: **The Loser Boozer**

IDENTIFYING REMARK: "Sorry, dude. I'm too frunk to duck."

IDENTIFYING BEHAVIOR: Parties seven nights a week; talks about partying seven nights a week; is a dud in the sack; has really bad breath from drinking, smoking, and booger sugar.

CLASSIFICATION: **The Grandson of Sam (aka "The Serial Killer")**

IDENTIFYING REMARK: "How do you feel about pain?"

IDENTIFYING BEHAVIOR: Guards his plate with a knife and fork; tells stories about torturing animals when he was little; has a temper that's easily triggered by weird things, like too much salt in his food or the color blue; insists that Manson got a bad rap; looks like the guy next door; knows too much about your shower routine.

CLASSIFICATION: **The Eye Candy**

IDENTIFYING REMARK: "Do you like my hair?"

IDENTIFYING BEHAVIOR: Stares blankly; giggles constantly; finds ingenious ways to check himself out in his silverware.

CLASSIFICATION: **The Two-Timing Tomcat**

IDENTIFYING REMARK: "What ring?"

IDENTIFYING BEHAVIOR: Can only see you on certain days; has a white strip on his wedding finger; seems in a hurry for sex; has monogrammed luggage.

CLASSIFICATION: **The Cell-Phone Addict**

IDENTIFYING REMARK: "Hold, please."

IDENTIFYING BEHAVIOR: Takes a call while you're on the date; makes a call when you're on the date; calls someone when you're stomping out the door; never calls again.

CLASSIFICATION: **The U.F.O. (Unidentified Foolish Operative)**

IDENTIFYING REMARK: "Have you ever been to Roswell?"

IDENTIFYING BEHAVIOR: Refers to himself as a 'droid; tries to flatter you by saying someone must have shot you with a phaser set on "hottie"; says he'd like to beam you up to his starship.

CLASSIFICATION: **The Bulldozer**

IDENTIFYING REMARK: "You know you like it."

IDENTIFYING BEHAVIOR: Orders "a nice rack" for dinner; introduces you as "my old lady"; asks your breasts what they do for a living.

CLASSIFICATION: **The Wet Noodle**

IDENTIFYING REMARK: "Sorry, I guess I'm a little tired."

IDENTIFYING BEHAVIOR: Lets you kiss him but pulls your hand away if you try to do more; waits for you to make all the first moves.

CLASSIFICATION: **The Home Boy**

IDENTIFYING REMARK: "I'd invite you in, but my parents are sleeping."

IDENTIFYING BEHAVIOR: Loves comic books; can't take you out because he has to do chores for his parents; probably plays in a band.

CLASSIFICATION: **The Cheap Bastard**

IDENTIFYING REMARK: "Does five sound OK? Happy hour ends at seven."

IDENTIFYING BEHAVIOR: Rushes ahead of you at the movies and buys his own ticket; says he has only $10 on him since he didn't have time to get his check cashed.

CLASSIFICATION: **The Adolescent**

IDENTIFYING REMARK: "What's your favorite video game?"

IDENTIFYING BEHAVIOR: Stays late at work to play PlayStation with other juvenile coworkers; takes pride in the length of his burps; tends to change fashion statements at the drop of a hat (from baggy pants and Caesar 'do to rock 'n' roll-tattooed-waif thing).

CLASSIFICATION: **The New Ager**

IDENTIFYING REMARK: "Your aura looks lovely tonight."

IDENTIFYING BEHAVIOR: Burns sage in your apartment before he goes out with you; tells you his spirit guide said that you would be "very special"; says your cat keeps smiling at him; introduces you as his "mystic lady"; has B.O.

CLASSIFICATION: **The Player**

IDENTIFYING REMARK: "Your mom is hot!"

IDENTIFYING BEHAVIOR: Offers the "best massage you've ever had in your life" before he even tells you his last name; used to date your sister; used to date your cousin; says he knows the best free clinic in town.

CLASSIFICATION: **The Stoner**

IDENTIFYING REMARK: "Boobs, doobs, and tube."

IDENTIFYING BEHAVIOR: Gets into discussions about who's better—the Stones or Zep; generally apathetic; likes to stimulate the brain without moving the body (listening to music, watching TV); explores the Web's innermost quadrants in an effort to find the most arcane sites; loves trivia.

Second Step: The Escape
BAD-DATE BREAKOUTS

Of course, once a truly bad date has been identified, a real woman knows how to get the hell out. Once you've established that you are indeed on a first-class lame date (rule of thumb: would you rather be doing your taxes?), you'll need to know the exit strategy that works for you.

1. THE WRAP-IT-UP

For dates that have zero chemistry but aren't entirely hellish.

This kind of date should be looked at as being in prison for just a short sentence. You suffer for a designated period of time (15, 30, or 60 minutes— long enough to be civil, short enough to keep from getting hostile), then cut out with an excuse and an apology.

Bad Date Tip #2

When stuck on a bad date, some of us find it useful to chat up hotties when our date's back is turned (being the resourceful types that we are). It's a little ego boost, not to mention a way to meet someone you really like. We fully recommend this, but only if you can do it on the sly.

The Excuse

> "I have a huge presentation due tomorrow and need to work on it."
>
> "I completely forgot that I have to drop some important papers off at my folks' house, and they go to bed at nine. Sorry."

2. THE RUNAWAY

For more serious situations, like psychos and body builders.

Excuse yourself and head for the ladies' room. Call a friend, tell her to wait 15 minutes, then call the restaurant (or wherever you are) and have you paged. If you can't reach your friend, nab your server and clue them in—they'll gladly participate in your scheme if only to alleviate the tedium of waiting tables (see Greasing the Palm). If you brought your own car, apologize, pay for whatever you've ordered, and make a run for it. If you came with your date, ask your friend (or your new friend the server) to call a cab for you so it's waiting outside. (Your date will think it was coincidence.) If a cab's not an option (see Bad Date Tip #1), you'll have to ask your date to take you home pronto.

The Excuse

> "I feel really nauseous [probably not a complete lie] and have to leave now!" Tip: Clutch your stomach for extra emphasis. Also, if you tell him you feel like you're gonna throw up, there's no way your date will want to come in.

3. THE FREAKOUT

For dates that are so unbearably dull, you need to shock just for the thrill of it.

If you find yourself so bored that you can't even remember your date's name, it's time to employ this surefire date-repellent. Bring up a topic that will guarantee a quick wrap-up to the evening. Tip: The more creative you are with these conversational bombs, the more fun you'll have. For instance, "It's so nice to be on a date since my boyfriend got locked up—good thing he gets out tomorrow," or "Geez, my herpes is really bothering me tonight."

EVIL LANDLORD

mission:
**To keep your tenant-landlord relationship
free of ill will, serious conflict, or letter-bombs.**

When the roaches in your apartment become more like roommates than occasional visitors (bad sign: when you begin to name them), who are you gonna call? The landlord, and usually he or she will take care of the problem. But this section isn't about those landlords. It's about the other kind—the ones who make you want to fake your own death just to get out of your lease. So learn how to protect yourself from this insidious adversary.

Your landlord is required to keep your unit in habitable condition. Here's what that means:

1. A sound building structure, including floors, roofs, and stairways.
2. Safe electrical, heating, and plumbing systems.
3. A reasonable supply of hot and cold water.
4. Terminating a pest infestation. Of course, if the problem is a

result of your sloppy living habits (like leaving trails of Krispy Kreme doughnut crumbs from the kitchen to the TV), you will foot the bill.

For problems like mildewed grout, broken blinds, or peeling paint—in other words, stuff that won't kill you but is a major decor drag—your landlord may or may not have an obligation to fix them. Always check:

1. your lease to see if the terms agree to maintaining these types of repairs.
2. state and local building codes.
3. landlord-tenant laws.
4. any promises your landlord has made, either verbal or written.

Fact: Landlords will NOT change the color of your carpet from industrial gray to ivory shag. **Cosmetic changes are not their deal.**

Minor repair problems? Here's the beef. *Note: These tactics are for evil landlords only. If your landlord is the type who will fix things without being harassed, threatened, or begged, thank your lucky stars. You must have done something nice in a past life.*

And now for the serious stuff . . .

1. WRITE A LETTER

Clearly state the nature of the problem, focusing on why it's in your landlord's best interest to take care of it. Speak in a language he understands—Cash Money. In other words, if he doesn't take care of the hole in the carpet, someone could trip and hurt herself, leaving him open to a fat lawsuit. Or the peeling paint in the bathroom could eventually turn into a mildewed wall, which means replacing the whole

Evil Landlord Tip #1

In some states, tenants are allowed to deduct the amount of a repair from their rent. But check the laws carefully before resorting to this tactic. It's strictly a last-ditch attempt to force the Evil One into action. Once you've established you're within your rights to withhold the rent, write the landlord to inform him that this is your plan. Then head to the local courthouse and file the necessary papers for withholding the rent. Deposit the rent in an escrow account maintained by the court or a mediating service. Tip: Keeping the rent there—rather than going to Barney's and depositing it in the "new shoes account"—will look better to a judge.

damn thing down the road. If the problem affects other tenants, make the landlord aware of it. The advantage of writing a letter is that the landlord is less likely to automatically say, "Forget it!" Plus, you've got a paper trail.

2. HAVE A LITTLE TALK

If your letters and telephone calls are ignored, contact a mediation service. You can find them in the yellow pages under, um, "Mediation Services." This is a less expensive alternative to going to court, since many community mediators are free—or almost free. This process works pretty much the same way it did when you were a kid and your mom "mediated" your more hysterical sibling conflicts. (Except without the screeching. At least not as much.) The three of you will sit down, you'll tell your side of the story (just the facts, please), and your landlord will tell his. In a perfect world, the mediator will then tell the landlord what a cretin he is, and you'll be completely vindicated. Since this is a far-from-perfect world, chances are he'll come up with a fair compromise.

3. SEE YOU IN SMALL CLAIMS

Obviously, this is a worst-case solution. The reality is, once the relationship between you and your evil landlord has moved into court, you probably won't

Check to make sure your state has anti-retaliation laws. These prohibit a landlord from retaliating for your complaints with crappy "paybacks" like hiking the rent or even eviction.

want to live in your place any-more. But if you really want to stay in your apartment—if it's rent-controlled, for example—you may have to fight it out. The lowdown: If you can prove that your unit's value has decreased due to the lack of repairs, a judge may find in your favor. This doesn't mean you'll be sailing to the Riviera on a big, fat judgment. Rather, the award will be determined by sub-tracting the monthly amount your unit is actually worth from what you've been pay-ing for rent since you've had the problem. You get the difference.

Search Me?

Landlords have the right to enter your apartment in the following situations:
· if there's an emergency,
· to make repairs, or
· to show the apartment to prospective tenants.
Most states require a 24-hour notification if the landlord wants to enter the apartment. Landlords may not enter your apartment to water your plants, check to see if you have enough to eat, or make your bed.

How to Break Your Lease

Obviously, a lease is a written contract specifying, among other things, that you will stay in your apartment for a specific period of time. So how do you get out of it?

* If your landlord significantly violates the lease, you can break it.

* Some states have laws that allow a tenant to break a lease for health

reasons or job relocation. So if you want to break the lease in order to get a bigger and better apartment in another part of town, lie! Tip: Crying while lying sometimes helps your case.

Note: Often it's easy for the landlord to re-rent the apartment right away—especially if you help line up a new tenant. So breaking your lease may turn out to be a breeze.

FIRST CLASS

mission:
**To find airfare that's cheap enough to have money
left over for cocktails on the plane.**

Nothing gets us high like soaring 35,000 feet above ground
on cut-rate airfare. Getting a bargain-basement fare is a tricky business,
and navigating the world of discount fares takes some primo hustling skills.

When can you get discounted fares? When you travel:

1. For a funeral or for a family emergency. Like to see a close relative
   who's suddenly fallen ill. Airlines call them "sympathy" fares and
   will drop rates as low as 50% to 70% ; ask to speak with a
   manager if the reservations agent says they don't offer them.
2. For a wedding. Airlines will give bulk discount rates for out-
   of-town guests.
3. As a student. Be prepared to show an ID (see First Class).
4. With a senior citizen. You can get a discount, but this only
   works for one accompanying passenger.

The Courier Caper

If you have a flexible schedule, don't mind traveling light, and are into exploring new destinations on your own, consider being a courier. Airfares are rock-bottom cheap (sometimes free), and you can travel to exotic locales like Europe, Australia, South America, Asia, and Africa.

THE DEAL:

When you act as a courier, you accompany air freight and make sure it gets delivered to an air courier representative once you reach the destination. You can book flights in advance, or save even more $$$ by being able to leave at the last moment. You need to live near a major city (Los Angeles, Chicago, New York, San Francisco, or Miami), be 18, and have a passport.

THE HOW-TO:

Student Travel Sites
Council Travel
(www.counciltravel.com)
Smarter Living for Students
(www.smarterliving.com/student)
STA Travel
(www.sta-travel.com)

To become a courier, you have to pay an annual membership fee (usually under $50) to a company that has access to courier flight information.

DID YOU KNOW?

If you checked in on time and are involuntarily bumped from your flight, you are eligible for compensation. If the airline puts you on another flight (same airline or different one) that gets you to your destination between one and two hours later than your originally scheduled flight, you're entitled to compensation (usually flight vouchers) equal to the price of your one-way fare, up to a maximum of $200. More than two hours late? That maximum doubles to $400.

Scams We Love—and Airlines Hate!

SCAM #1: THE FLY-THROUGH

If you're trying to get from point A to point B, you may not want to buy a ticket from point A to point B. Do some research: You might save money if you buy a ticket that goes from point A to C, with a "pit stop" at point B. It's a sneaky little move called a "fly-through" that the savviest flyers know and love. *Note: It does violate the regulations of some airlines, so be sure to check the fine print.*

Courier Organizations
Air Courier Association
(www.aircourier.org)
Jupiter Air (www.jupiterair.com)
International Association of
Air Travel Couriers
(www.courier.org)

SCAM #2: MERCI BEAUCOUP!

If you're flying to Europe for a wildly glamorous adventure, instead of flying from, say, Los Angeles to London round-trip, book a departing flight from L.A. to London and (here's the sneaky part) a returning flight from Paris to Los Angeles. In other words, fly into one city and out of another. (It's called flying "open jaws.") You may save some moolah (especially if the U.S. dollar is stronger than the currency in the country where you bought your ticket), and avoid unnecessary extra traveling costs. *Trés* smart.

FRIENDSHIP FIXES

mission:
To manage your friendships with kindness,
tolerance, and the occasional whack upside the head.

Friends can bring fun, excitement, and impromptu road
trips to one's life. (We love impromptu road trips.) That's the good stuff.
We also know they can bring annoying habits, stupid spats, and pesky
complications, too. Yes, as with all good things, there's a price to pay for
the company of a quality sidekick. Here's how to manage a few of the
most classic friendship flare-ups.

HOW TO: **Go Separate Ways**

SCENARIO: You grew up with Tonya. But as you've grown older, she's
begun to morph into the kind of chick who wears headbands and quotes
Oprah, while you just got your third body part pierced. Clearly, you and
Tonya have grown apart. It's time to let you both off the hook.

Dumping a Friend in 3 Easy Steps

1. Talk to Tonya one-on-one. Never give the heave-ho by telephone or (worse) by leaving a message or (the worst!) by sending an e-mail.
2. Tell Tonya you feel like the relationship isn't working. Give her specific examples (without being nasty—no need to be insulting), as well as a chance to respond.
3. If you still want out once you've talked awhile, tell her you think it's best if you take a break from each other for a little while.

Friendship Fix Tip #1

Not all friends will be Ethel to your Lucy. Sometimes we do grow apart and want to do a little spring cleaning. Don't torture yourself about it—hey, chances are she's tired of you, too.

HOW TO: **Get Her Back**

SCENARIO: Crap. You've just made a spectacular, vodka-inspired mistake that involved your buddy's studly ex, four Jell-O shots, and a long night that ended with you and Mr. Stud Guy watching the sun come up from a chaotic backseat. (When you make a mistake, you do it big.) Now, in the bitter light of day and an epic hangover, you realize it's time to seriously sweet-talk your friend. Here's how:

Winning a Friend Back in 5 Easy Steps

1. Call your friend and tell her you've made a hideous, mind-boggling boo-boo. (No, not the one about losing your shoes the night before. That was a different mistake.) Tell her exactly what you did (blurt it out fast, before you lose your nerve). Follow up by saying that you're sorry. Sorrier than you've ever been, in fact.
2. What you say next depends on how she reacts. If she hasn't hung up on you, tell her you realize that you've hurt her

and you hate that more than anything. Then ask to get together to talk.

3. Be sincere. Master the art of being apologetic without groveling. (If that doesn't work, go ahead and grovel.)

4. Don't expect her to forgive you right away. Recognize that her feelings may not have healed yet—give her time.

5. Sending flowers never hurts.

> **Friendship Fix Tip #2**
> We never dump our coconspirators for a lover. Hotties come and go, but best friends can scheme together for a lifetime.

HOW TO: **Tell a Friend Something She Doesn't Want to Hear**

SCENARIO: You and Juanita watch each other's backs. But lately you feel like she's turned into a real downer. She complains nonstop and backstabs your other friends. Frankly, the girl's bad mood is driving you crazy.

Tell a Friend She's Bugging You in 3 Easy Steps

1. Use the old "Sugar First" strategy. Before you slam your friend, tell her what you do like about her. Tell her that you love hanging out with her but that you have to talk with her about something that's bugging you.

2. Tell her what's on your mind, and be specific: "Janelle, did you really have to throw up on my mom at graduation?"

3. Prepare yourself—this is the part where she may go off, usually by becoming defensive. On the other hand, she may cop to what she's doing. Or she could make a case that completely justifies her behavior. Either way, listen to what she has to say and tell her you hope the two of you can work things out.

Score Tickets
9am
Be early!
Wow, sometimes the box office has extra tickets!
Box Office
Ticket
ticket!
or Call a Ticket Broker
Hello, Mr. Ticket Broker here. May I help you?
Listen to the Radio
AM
FM

FRONT ROW

mission:
To get great seats without doing anything stupidly expensive or scuzzy.

Whether it's a U2 concert or a Lakers game, one thing's for sure—it's a lot harder these days to score the Sweet Seats. Security is tighter and tickets are beyond the budget of anyone without a trust fund. That's why, like so many other things in life, getting a good seat has everything to do with who you know.

Hence, these few simple tips for getting tickets. It's a dirty job, but somebody's gotta do it.

Tactical Maneuvers
SHOP THE BOX OFFICE

Always shop the box office before you hit TicketMaster. With TM, you'll be suckered for all kinds of "service" charges that'll send your $15 ticket price to the shy side of $30 in no time. Also, the box office will sometimes release extra tickets the day of the show.

SHOW UP THE SAME DAY AS THE BIG EVENT

For most major shows, there is almost always someone

* whose date didn't show up,
* who is a member of the press and has an extra ticket, or
* who won tickets on the radio and had to go alone.

Your chances for scoring this free ticket are always better when you're alone (although sometimes there is strength in numbers—two of you can work opposite ends of the venue).

CALL THE BROKER

If you must be in the front row of the show, try a ticket broker. Find a reputable one through the National Association of Ticket Brokers (www.natb.org). Or shop around with local brokers, since they usually have long-term contracts with nearby venues. Just don't be a total sucker—call at least three brokers, since prices will vary.

TRY THE RADIO

Listen to your favorite local radio station to win tickets.

LAST POSSIBLE RESORT

Learn how to write reviews (free is OK, but paying is better) for a weekly newspaper, Web site, magazine, whatever, and score tickets through your press contacts. This routine has kept many a poorly paid freelance writer from seriously hating life.

THE INTERMISSION SCAM

This is a sneaky way to see a big show—or, at least, half of one—for free. Here's the drill: Turn up for the show after it begins, then, when everyone comes out at intermission, mingle with the crowd. Walk back inside the theater with the crowd when they return to the seats. Now find some empty seats to plop down in— ushers almost never check tickets on the way back! This trick works for operas, ballets, and other upscale events, too. Just be sure to wear your fancy duds, not your torn jeans, so you fit in with the swells.

One caveat: This scam is not for the ethically squeamish or the easily embarrassed. Technically, it's illegal. While you're not likely to be thrown in jail if you're caught, you will probably be thrown out of the theater.

GREASE THE PALM

mission:
To learn the subtle art of persuasive payola.

When a customer eats a meal in a restaurant, she *tips* the server when paying the bill. When she signs up for cable and decides she wants all the premium channels for the low, low price of free, she *bribes* the cable guy. Tipping requires common sense, but bribing requires real style.

Tipping Tactics

The following tips are the minimum you should leave in various situations. If your server has really gone above and beyond, let your conscience be your guide. *Note: Rules for tipping in other countries may differ. Always check before you assume.*

ALWAYS TIP THE:

• Waiter, waitress, and headwaiter: Serving people in a restaurant is a hellish job and one that most of us have endured. We recommend you always tip 20%, unless the service is lousy (defined by completely forgetting your order, as opposed to bringing you the wrong wine); then you can tip 10%. But never stiff your waiter completely—these people survive on their tips.

The point here is that **it doesn't cost much to be generous.** Will it really kill you to give a buck or two to the lady in the bathroom?

- Bartender and wine steward: 15%
- Checkroom attendant: $1 per coat, or $2 for extra stuff like packages, umbrellas, briefcases, etc.
- Washroom attendant: 50¢–$2, depending on the service they provide.
- Strolling musicians in restaurants: $1 a song per musician (three songs played by three musicians would cost you $9).
- Valet: $2.
- Hotel doorman: $1–$2 if they give your bags to the bellman; $1–$3 for summoning a taxi; $1–$2 for bringing your car to the door.
- Hotel bellman: $1 per bag, especially if they bring it to your room.
- Hotel maid: $2 per night per person in large hotel; $1 per night per person in small hotel. Leave in an envelope that says "Housekeeping" if you can't find him or her in person.
- Room-service waiter: Tip just like any other waiter.
- Concierge: $5 minimum for handling airline or theater reservations; $10 if they go above and beyond the call of duty (like getting you tickets to Siegfried & Roy).
- Skycap: $1 per bag.
- Taxi driver: 20% of the fare; more if they go out of their way for you (e.g., carrying your bags to your front door).
- Hair colorist, masseuse or masseur, hairstylist, aromatherapist, facialist, makeup artist, aesthetician, nail technician: 15-20% of the fee.
- Shampoo person: $1–$3.
- Car-washer: $2–$3.

- Garage attendant: $1.
- Grocery loader: $1–$2, depending on the number of bags he or she takes to your car and loads.
- Cleaning staff, baby-sitter: Holiday tips of $10-$25 and a personal gift.

The Basics of Bribing

Good for siblings, cable guys, some employees in foreign countries, and the occasional ex-lover.

When traveling, carry lots of ones. Cash a twenty before you even head to the airport, and, voilà, there's your tip fund. Take note of this travel advice from a particularly savvy (just slightly pampered) Traveler: **"Never carry anything heavier than a dollar bill."**

1. Never, ever offer money to a cop. This is illegal and could land you in jail. Can you say "slammer" en Español?
2. Bribing requires the keen skills of a good listener. If the potential bribee is trying to resolve a situation, wait until there's an opening in the conversation; then ask if there's a quicker or more efficient way to work out the situation.
3. Only offer what you can afford to pay (i.e., don't tell your sister you'll loan her your Anna Sui sweater if it actually belongs to your best friend).
4. Never say this: "If I give you five bucks, will you let me cut to the front of the line?" Try this instead: "This is a really long line, and I have to get back to work before my boss fires me. Would ten dollars move me any closer to the front?"
5. And don't forget: Payola comes in many forms besides cold cash—sometimes favors, goods, or services make excellent bribes.

Bribing Your Friends

If you ask your friends to do you a big favor (like paint your apartment), they deserve a reward. Tell them you'll buy pizzas and beer. **Tip: Never offer something and then fail to deliver.** Talk is cheap, and you will be, too!

GROOVEABLE FEAST

mission:

To throw a bash where no one gets arrested, or a dinner party
where no one gets a) bored or b) food poisoning.

Of course, we know you know how to party. But we're talking
about more than another debauched night on the town. We're talking
about your skills at throwing a semi-grown-up soiree—the kind without a
keg or police intervention. A smashing party is the mark of a true adult—a
real coming-of-age ritual that can win you friends, clients, and a few interesting new phone numbers.

A successful fete can be broken down into three simple components:

1. Guests
2. Ambience
3. Food and Drink

Let's review them all.

Guests

FOR THE BLOWOUT: The trick to a blowout is volume, so invite everyone you know, and tell them the more the merrier. More importantly—invite your neighbors. If they don't come, the cops probably will later.

FOR THE INTIMATE GATHERING. Invite people who will work together socially. Think of people who might be interesting to one another but who aren't too much alike. So if all your friends are actors, we're sorry. Just kidding. Be sure to invite at least a couple of guests who have more to talk about than their last audition rejection.

FOR THE DINNER PARTY: Don't seat the rabid atheist next to the pious Catholic, unless you like the idea of food fights around your table.

Ambience

Music is key. Always have a great selection of tunes (CDs or mix tapes) playing. *Never* play the radio. There's nothing worse than hearing ads blasting over cocktail conversation.

Set the mood with lighting. The best party-givers despise naked lightbulbs. Cover yours with paper Chinese balloons or Indian/Tibetan folding screens. String little white strands of Xmas lights or kitsch ones (like chili peppers or animals) over doorways. Put candles everywhere (yummy ones made with essential oil are great but keep them far from where people are eating). Tiki torches set a perfect tropical mood for outdoor parties.

Scent is seductive and instantly arouses good vibes in your guests. Burn incense (not too sweet but interesting, like Black Love or Nag Champa). Place sweet-smelling flowers (like lilies, narcissus, roses) around in small bunches.

Your seating set-up often determines the mood of a party. Big, comfy pillows give a loungy feel to your room. Lots of chairs tell people you expect it to be a mellow gathering. And of course, clear a big space for dancing if you want people to boogie down.

Food and Drink

Keep the drinks flowing. Whether

you're juicin' 40s or sipping sparkling cider, there should always be enough to drink. Tip: Make sure you have two blenders for dueling margaritas.

Where there is drink, there should always be food. Nibbles include salty snacks (like olives or nuts), chicken wings, chips and salsa, shrimp cocktail, hummus and pitas, and cheese and crackers. With all due respect to Martha, making a gazillion different appetizers is way too time-consuming. If you live near a Trader Joe's or a Costco, they sell great assortments of frozen hors d'oeuvres.

It's always fun to introduce a drink du jour. Hence the Love Grenade. It'll have them lining up. Fill a blender about halfway with ice cubes. Then add one part Southern Comfort and two parts orange juice. Blend, then pour into glasses. Float a splash of Grand Marnier on top, then light it. (Make sure to use a long lighter-wand.)

If you are cooking for your shindig, don't get too complicated. On a date, for example, don't serve student food (spaghetti with tomato sauce), but don't bust out the paté, either. Make a dish you feel confident cooking. Or get your guests to help you cook. Note: This is a gamble, since there are some guests who like to watch, rather than cook.

faboo appetizers → Sushi ← shrimp ← olives

65

The Occasion	The Music
Big Bash/Shake Your Booty	Everyone loves disco; mix current music with oldies (like Moby with the *Carwash* sound track). Or play the music that makes your group nostalgic. It could be '80s tunes (Blondie, The Smiths, Bauhaus, New Order), late '70s punk rock (The Ramones, Sex Pistols, The Clash), or old-school hip-hop (Grandmaster Flash, Whodini, Roxanne Shante).
Small Sit-Down Dinner Party	You want the evening to have an **Eclectic & Mellow** sultry groove (Miles Davis, Cesaria Evora, Buena Vista Social Club, Nightmares on Wax, Thievery Corporation, Massive Attack, Bebel Gilberto).
A Date/Getting to Know You	The music should reflect who you are without being intrusive (Serge Gainsbourg—especially with Brigitte Bardot—vintage Dolly Parton, Spain, Chet Baker, etc.).
Booty Call/Butt Naked	Whatever gets your motor running (D'Angelo)!

Don't leave your antique heirloom diamond necklace lying out. **Hide all your valuables**, and put breakables someplace safe. Why tempt fate or the infrequent sticky-fingered party guest?

How to Create a Boomin' Buffet

* In terms of decor, think big (bowls, baskets, large quantities of food) and bold colors (like red, black, and gold for a Chinese-themed table). Go to town on decorations when it comes to your buffet.

* Always have a focal point for the buffet. It doesn't have to be a fussy centerpiece. Try an overflowing

basket (filled with something that sets a theme) at the end of the table.

* A table filled with flat trays and small food doesn't look like much. Arrange food at various heights and angles to give the table some drama.

Bonus Party Advice—the Flip Side
HOW TO GET OUT OF A LAME PARTY

There's nothing worse than getting dressed up for a night out on the town only to get to your fabulous fete and find out it's a funeral in disguise. When you find it necessary to cut out right after you've arrived, relax. Have a drink (free booze!), then find your host or hostess and explain that a) you have cramps or b) you have to get up early tomorrow morning or c) you had a really long day and are exhausted. Then beat it.

Hostess jitters are as common as late guests. Don't stress. Your job is to welcome people and **enjoy the fun**.

HIGHWAY TO HELL

mission:
To keep your driving rap sheet short and sweet.

There's something about getting behind the wheel that makes us all giddy inside. It's a car thing. It's a freedom thing. How else are we supposed to tail people? On foot? In platforms? Ha!

Driving Maneuvers Your High School Teacher Never Told You About
THE DUI BLUES
Driving after you've been drinking goes against the rule of smart babes everywhere. In case you're unclear on this point, let's review it in big, bold letters: Real women DO NOT drink and drive. Sure, there's a difference between having one cocktail and having four, but here's a reality check— you are considered legally impaired long before you actually feel drunk. So don't be stupid. If you drink, call a cab or hitch a ride with a friend.

Do you know the clues to help you size up this situation?

Never, ever drive with empties in your car. If a cop spots them, he automatically has reason to search your car and give you a sobriety test.

BAD SCENARIO:

It's Gail's birthday, and after two hours of partying after work, she leaves the Kasbah to drive home in her '69 Chevy Camaro. Gail figures since she only had one glass of champagne and three Cosmopolitans, she's okay to drive. Problem is, she also had a fight with her boyfriend, Raffi, so Gail's really not paying a lot of attention to the road. After straddling the lane while lighting a cigarette, weaving while trying to find decent music on the radio, and taking an extra-wide turn*, she hears the unmistakable sound of a police siren right behind her. Gail pulls over and waits for Officer Big Stick to approach her.

Gail has obviously never thought twice about a little something called blood alcohol content (BAC). It stands for the amount of alcohol that's found in your bloodstream, and cops measure it to determine whether you're over the legal limit (which varies from state to state). In most states, you are considered legally drunk when your BAC is .08 (that's 8%) or higher. Problem is, no one wants to go to the trouble of calculating his or her BAC while standing at the Tiki bar.

*Cops are on the lookout for drunk drivers, and sloppy moves like a wide turn tip them off that you are three sheets to the wind.

So here's a rule of thumb: If you're driving, never drink more than one drink per hour, and never more than three drinks in one outing. (If you're smaller than average—less than 120 pounds—your limit should really be two drinks.)

To be more conservative, alternate your drinks: one beer, then a soft drink, etc. To understand how BAC works, let's take Gail as an example. She weighs 130 pounds and had four drinks—probably very strong drinks, too. (Cosmos are usually on the boozy side.) In other words, Gail's in trouble.

CUI—Crying Under the Influence

Avoid drinking + driving + crying. It's a fact that the effects of alcohol are intensified when you are in an emotional state. We've heard of an Operative in the middle of a breakup who puked all night after drinking one beer. When you're freaking out, drown your sorrows at home, or even better, down a soothing, hot drink (superrich hot chocolate with fat marshmallows can hit the spot).

Gail's about to face The Man. What should she do?
* First, she should pop an Altoids in her mouth. It's not proven, but there's a strong rumor that these powerhouse mints not only help cover up the smell of alcohol on your breath but can screw up the Breathalyzer results, too.
* Deny, deny, deny. Under no circumstances should Gail tell Officer Big Stick that she's been drinking. He will not care if she's had only one drink, and any admission of imbibing will give him more reason to make Gail walk the line.
* If Gail is a good liar, she should have a story ready about where she really was. ("Officer, I've been at work since six this morning and am just now going home. I'm exhausted.")
* In some states, you can object to taking a Breathalyzer test, request the one you want to take, or respectfully request to have an attorney present before you answer any questions. In other states, you can't.

One more time: Don't drive after drinking.

Highway Patrol Tip #2
Do not behave like people on Cops if you get pulled over. Always be courteous and respectful (in other words, bite your tongue), and have your driver's license and registration in a handy spot.

Speeding Tickets

Until you're having fun, fun, fun on the Autobahn, you have to drive slow, slow, slow in the States. That doesn't mean you should crawl at 55 miles per hour when everyone else is cruising at 70. That's just a good way to get flipped the bird by your friendly fellow drivers. Keeping up with the speed of traffic is key and usually safer. (Slow cars sometimes actually cause accidents.) In general, you can drive 5 to 8 miles per hour over the speed limit on highways. On streets, don't go more than 5 over the limit if you want to stay out of speeding ticket school. And never speed in a school zone—that will get you in real trouble, not to mention brand you a real jerk.

Ticket Tactics

1. When speeding, keep in mind that if you are pulled over and the cop finds you were sailing by at 15 miles per hour above the speeding limit, you'll get hit with major fines and insurance hikes. So if you were speeding at 70 miles per hour in a 55 miles per hour zone, try to talk the cop down a mile. A ticket stating you were only 14 miles per hour over the speeding limit will keep you on this side of the "Dangerous Driver" line.

2. Ditch the Police Union decal. You should support the police because you want to, not

because you think it'll save you from a speeding ticket. A bumper sticker never saved anyone from getting busted.

3. Down South they call it "pork bait." OK, it's a terrible name, but it describes those folks who fly past everyone else. If you speed, set your cruise control to go slower than the PB who's just rocketed past you at 80 mph. Hopefully, that guy will be the one who gets pulled over instead of you.

4. In some areas, there are posted signs stating that the speed limit is enforced by aircraft. We've never known anyone to get a ticket from a cop in an airplane. Use your own discretion.

Highway Patrol Tip #5

If you speed past a cop and your eyes meet, give a friendly nod and carefully but quickly step on the brakes. This way, you're letting him know you're trying to correct the "situation." If he decides to pursue you, pull over immediately. Cops don't like to chase anyone, and an irate cop means hard times for you.

HIT THE ROAD

mission:

To be fully prepared for a break for the border (or for the closest mai-tai-soaked resort town) at all times.

If you're the traveling-adventuress type, this section was written for you. We know your wanderlusting kind—you live for new countries, new experiences, and new, non-English-speaking hotties. While others sit and daydream, you're booking the next getaway to an exotic beach, wild safari, or road trip to the next town with a day spa. To make your travel fantasy come true (except for the part about that surfer guy), you need only two things: a See Ya Sucker Stash and a properly packed Bug-Out Bag. Remember: With careful planning, you, too, could spend that summer in Greece with just a bathing suit bottom and a few good books. Okay, a few trashy books.

See Ya Sucker Stash
Want to know the biggest obstacle between you and that life-changing trip to Belize? Here's a hint: It's not finding someone to go with or getting the

time off work. Nope, as is true for so many things in life, it's *cash*—the cold hard stuff—and lots of it. Consider this:

Pricey vs. Priceless

A pair of Jimmy Choo shoes	vs.	airfare to France
An expensive dinner at Le Swanque Café	vs.	a week's worth of meals on the beach in Sri Lanka
A new work outfit (yawn!)	vs.	a few nights in a sleepy seaside town in Mexico
An annual gym membership (double yawn!)	vs.	a monthlong trek through Nepal

So go to your bank, open a brand-spanking-new savings account, and call it the See Ya Sucker Stash. Then make a point of putting some cash in it every week. The amount can be a little ($20) or a lot. Keep your savings book in a plastic bag, along with colorful travel brochures to your dream destinations, and stick it in the deep freeze (the refrigerator). Take it out only to register your deposits or when you're ready to take a trip. But that's all you're allowed to take it out for. Period. No ifs, ands, or buts. Got it? Good.

Note: We know of a traveling girl who keeps at least five changes of clothes in the trunk of her car. Do not turn into this person. **Sometimes too much preparedness is a bad thing.**

The Bug-Out Bag

One of the marks of a superior traveler is adaptability. And for maximum adaptability, we recommend you go out and get yourself a Bug-Out Bag. The BOB is like your purse, but better. It's the first thing you grab when you've gotta hit the road fast.

10 Essential Items for a Bug-Out Bag

The rest is up to you!

1. Lavender oil. Good for cuts, a stress-relieving bath, a peaceful sleep, or masking the smell of a rank gas-station bathroom.

2. A journal and pencil with sharpener. It's important to stoke your creativity and an awareness of your surroundings.

3. Unlubed condoms. For obvious reasons, but also when placed inside a sock, they can hold up to a liter of water.

4. Small tube of lube. Also for obvious reasons.

5. Dried fruit, like apricots or bananas, and Luna bars. Especially useful for quick energy boosts and in airports where the food is more dangerous than any "mechanical problem."

6. Slouchy hat and stylin' sunglasses. For a quick, low-key (not to mention wildly fashionable) disguise.

7. A Swiss Army knife with a beer/wine bottle opener, can opener, nail file, scissors, and tweezers.

8. Favorite paperback that you don't mind rereading.

9. Mini-makeup bag. It should contain tinted lip balm; sunscreen with 15 SPF; mascara; soothing eye gel; and triple-duty lipstick in a shade that works for lips, cheeks, and eyes (for when you need to change your identity fast).

10. Tissue packs. Wipe your butt, hands, nose, mouth, whatever. . . .

The Ultimate Globetrotter's Book List

For some of us, it's Jackie Collins or bust. But when you're hankering for something with a wandering theme, check out one of the following books:

Desert Places or *Tracks* by Robyn Davidson

Robyn kicks ass! Walking 1,700 miles across the Australian desert with only four camels and her dog for company and crossing the desert in India. She writes about it all—and herself—candidly, no matter how ugly it gets.

On the Road by Jack Kerouac

Okay, begrudgingly listed since the gals in it go nowhere. Despite this, it's damn good. A cross-country hitchhiking tale that some say has changed their lives.

Maiden Voyage by Tania Aebi

Your basic barfly-turned-world-traveler story. Tania's life changed when her dad offered her a college education or a 26-foot sailing ship. Duh! She sailed around the world by herself for two and a half years— and she was only 18.

West with the Night by Beryl Markham

This spectacular memoir is based on Beryl's life in Kenya, where she became an African bush pilot and the first person to fly solo across the Atlantic from east to west.

The Teachings of Don Juan: A Yaqui Way of Knowledge by Carlos Castaneda

OK, so it's a little out there for a travel book. Just think of it as a different kind of trip.

Out of Africa by Isak Dinesen
A love story between a Danish aristocrat and Kenya—not Robert Redford. Great writing, and miles better than the hokey movie.

Islands in the Clouds by Isabella Tree
A very cool story about Isabella's journeys to the remote Highlands of Papua New Guinea and Irian Jaya—one of the most dangerous regions on Earth.

The Beach by Alex Garland
A boy-style thriller set in Thailand.

Travels with Charley: In Search of America by John Steinbeck
A camper, a poodle, and an amazing writer travel across America circa 1960. A lovely read, with many observations still poignantly true today—like those about rampant tourism. If he only knew. Great dog writing, too.

Drive: Women's True Stories from the Open Road Edited by Jeannie Goode
These refreshing essays come from women, young and old. What unites them? The open road, girl, where they find many adventures and do a little inner tripping to boot.

HOME FOR THE HOLIDAYS

mission:

**To survive your next family reunion without
anybody getting hurt and/or disowned**

It's a fact of life that the longer you're away from your family, the more you imagine how fun it is to spend time with them (conveniently forgetting the last 26 painful occasions). The dream: a cozy holiday get-together with your loved ones. The reality: Dad planted in front of a blaring TV. Your sibs squabbling over some childhood grievance, then turning on anyone who tries to intervene. Mom refusing to come out of her bedroom. Old Uncle Marv telling that story about the saucy Italian honey he romanced during WWII. Aunt Pearl "accidentally" dropping her hot tea in Uncle Marv's lap. And you bolting to your car for a quick getaway.

Sound familiar? We thought so. Don't despair—consider these temper-saving tips before blowing up over the Thanksgiving turkey.

The Tactics

No matter how your family treats you, you are in control of your own reactions. That's right, nobody is making you fling the turkey at your brother-in-law's fat head. Furthermore, your sister doesn't make you wish she'd never been born; rather, you are choosing to have this nasty (albeit satisfying) thought all on your own. Once you realize that you are in charge of your emotions, you'll start to look twice at the stuff that really chaps your butt (a psychological term).

* Notions of right and wrong have no place in family politics. If you focus on what's fair, you'll be bitter for the rest of your life. So what if you spent two years of your teenage life grounded while your bratty kid brother partied until daybreak? Let it go. (Besides, you can always make up for lost time.)

* Be realistic about your expectations of other people. Is it fair—or realistic—to expect your grandma to appreciate the fine workmanship behind your latest tattoo?

What to Do When Good Parents Go Bad

If your parents say things that hurt your feelings, remember that their thoughtless behavior is something they learned, probably from another relative. Try to keep that reality check in mind before you lash out with a nasty comeback. Your grown-up behaviour may help them a) realize that they're being dolts and b) want to change. *Note: If they are abusive or physically harmful, do not subject yourself to their behavior. Get out and stay away until they've changed.*

Three Clues to Keeping Your Cool

Consider these things when talking with a family member, or anyone else for that matter.

Home for the Holidays Tip #2
Be sure to ask your older relatives questions about family history. It makes them feel good and has the added value of giving you excellent dirt on other relatives, especially your parents. This also gets high ratings for entertainment value at family functions.

* Don't yell. Your point will come across stronger if you speak in a normal tone. Yelling is ineffective anyway. (Yes, even when your Rush-Limbaugh-lovin' dad tells you that vegetarians are ruining the world.) It only brings real communication to a screeching stop. If you really disagree, change the subject.

* Perfect your timing. Learn to speak at the proper time, not when it's best for you.

* And no name-calling, either. You won't persuade anyone to see your side of the argument by getting personal. We know it is tempting to fall back on "Oh yeah, well, you're fat!" from time to time. (It's a classic!) But chances are it won't make your sister see your point about the defense budget.

Home for the Holidays Tip #3
If you let go of those nastier feelings you've got lurking inside—anger, hurt, resentment, and jealousy are the biggies— your world will be a much happier place, we promise. C'mon, are you really still peeved about your older sister selling your bike in fourth grade?

Home for the Holidays Tip #4
Get this into your stubborn head: There's no such thing as a "perfect" family. Ozzie and Harriet had a few knock-down-drag-outs, too. Accept your family members for who they are—not who you want them to be.

No name calling!

HOME REMEDY

mission:

**To cure your body and create kitchen
concoctions that would make Martha buy stock in YOUR company.**

A good Operative is never sloppy in her professional—or personal—habits. It's all in the details. Yes, we mean personal hygiene. Picture La Femme Nikita in her stilettos, training her telescopic lens on an unsuspecting target and letting out a huge belch. It just isn't a very compelling image.

Bad Breath

In high school, we had a teacher who midlecture would swig on a bottle of Listerine, walk to the window, open it, and spit. Yes, the dude was a freak. Even worse, his breath still stank. Guys like this you expect it from, but bad breath could never happen to you, right? *Right*. Read on, and learn how to battle your own bodacious breath.

Home Remedy Tip #1

If someone you know has bad breath, tell him or her tactfully. *Note: "Whoa! What died in your mouth?" isn't tactful.* It won't be easy, but your pal will probably be grateful. Be straightforward: "Carrie, I don't know if you realize it, but you're making a strong breath statement, and I thought you'd like to know before anyone else notices." *Note: This does not guarantee that the "stinker" won't get angry.* If you're the cowardly type, consider an anonymous phone call (or e-mail, if you're really scared). It will cost you, but *www.theyshouldknow.com* will contact the offender, then let you know how it went over, you big meanie.

THE CULPRITS

1. Stinky foods. Anchovies, garlic, blue cheese, pepperoni, salami, onions—yup, all that good stuff will make you reek.

2. Dry mouth. Medication, illness—like a cold, infection, upset stomach, or sinusitis—and dehydration can all cause dry mouth and give yours that funky taste and smell.

3. Dental drama. Gum disease and plaque are two very obvious culprits behind el stinko breatho.

4. Too much partying. Alcohol, tobacco, and drugs. Pucker up!

5. Menstrual cycle. Swelling gums = stinky breath.

6. Dieting or fasting. When you diet, your body breaks down stored fat and protein for fuel, all of which can add up to a scary breath situation.

THE CURE

1. Obviously, the quickest way to discover the source of your bad breath is to go to a dentist to make sure you don't have something lurking in your mouth.

2. If the dentist gives you the all-clear, adjust your diet, drink lots of water, and brush your teeth—and tongue—at least twice a day. Tip: Brushing your tongue, as well as your teeth, reduces mouth odor by 85%. You remove bacterial plaque, food debris, and dead cells.

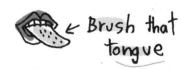

3. Floss every day, without fail.

4. Forget alcohol-based mouth-wash. Alcohol dries out your mouth tissues and causes them to secrete pungent plasma proteins. (Mmm, sweet, huh?) Instead, use a chloro-phyll-based mouthwash (available at most health food stores).

5. Chewing parsley, anise, fen-nel, or cloves after meals can also do the trick. Or try this bad-breath-busting potion: Mix 3 drops of peppermint oil, 1/2 cup of aloe vera juice, and 1/2 teaspoon of vegetable glycerin in a glass bottle. Shake well, and gargle whenever you think your breath is smelly. Tip: You can store this for up to a week as long as you keep it covered in a cool, dark place.

water + Sweet and Fresh = chlorophyll ← based mouthwash

Burping/Farting (It's a gas thing.)

Some gals get it when they're nervous; others when they've eaten too many beans. In turn-of-the-century France, a deadpan man named Pujol became very wealthy scandalizing and entertaining audiences with his master blaster act (only in France . . .).

THE CULPRITS

1. Swallowing air. Sure, we all breathe air, but when you eat or drink too fast, you will "come up" for air in between. So don't be a pig.

2. The breakdown of undigested foods. It's just like your mother always said: Take the time to let your food digest. Slow down, and don't jump up from the table right away.

THE CURE

1. Since swallowing air is the most common cause of gas, don't gobble your food or drinks (sometimes a problem for girls on the go). Chew slowly with your mouth closed. Sometimes breathing deeply for a minute before you start eating can help you relax while you chew.

2. Avoid carbonated drinks, chewing gum, and airy foods (whipped cream, soufflés). It makes sense when you think about it: The more air you take in, the more you'll let out.

3. Remember that farting is unavoidable. Apparently, it's normal to pass gas 14 to 23 times a day. (Turns out that excuse your ex used to give was true.) And as you've probably figured out, sometimes it stinks, sometimes it don't. It is also a supremely unfair fact that a healthy diet can cause a "gaseous situation." So if your diet is filled with stuff like dairy products, beans, fruits, vegetables, and whole grains, then good for you—but consider yourself warned.

4. Try this natural remedy for gas: Put a teaspoon of caraway seeds in a pan, cover with water, boil, and simmer for 10 minutes. Let your concoction cool, and sip it slowly before you eat. Alternatively, you could chew a few caraway seeds after a meal, drink a glass of warm water, and breathe deeply for 10 minutes.

5. Sip peppermint (for digestion) or chamomile (calming) tea after dinner.

6. Eat frequent small meals rather than three large ones.

7. To relax your esophagus muscles (and allow trapped gas to escape), put a drop of peppermint, ginger, or cinnamon extract (available at the health food store) in a cup of water, and sip it after a meal.

Yeast Infections

This is the most delicate of hygiene issues as well as the subject of countless moronic TV commercials. ("Sally, are you plagued by intimate itching?") The lowdown: Yeast infections are caused by an overgrowth of candida albicans, a fungus usually found in small quantities in the vaginal and intestinal tracts.

THE SYMPTOMS

1. A thick, white vaginal discharge with no odor.
2. A white coating of the vagina.

THE CULPRITS

1. Antibiotics. They kill bad and good bacteria.

2. Tight pants. Apologies to all the cha-cha's out there.

3. Hot bubble baths. We love 'em, but they don't always love us.

4. Nylon panties and pantyhose. Cotton panties and stockings are sexier anyway.

5. Feminine deodorant sprays and douches. These are just wrong. The chemicals in them can irritate your vagina as well as destroy its pH balance—learn to love your scent!

6. Hormones. Like those found in the Pill.

Fact: Men with yeast infections (yeah, they get 'em, too) may have an irritated and red penis or scrotum. Cute.

Cool Baths!

← cotton panties

7. Doing It. Unfortunately, yeast infections can be sexually transmitted.

8. A weakened immune system. Illness can cause yeast infections.

9. Too much sugar. Not only does the sweet stuff mess with your moods, but it also upsets your pH balance.

THE CURE

Over-the-counter methods cost a lot, and your body can become resistant to them. These natural remedies bring relief and are a lot cheaper.

1. Take nondairy acidophilus (healthy bacteria) capsules orally, or insert them into your vagina.

2. Eat lots of yogurt. Or better yet, take plastic tampon applicators and fill them with unsweetened, plain yogurt. Stick 'em in the freezer (or don't), and pop them into your vagina at night when you have an infection. The coolness will feel great and help to relieve that burning yeastie. Tip: Be sure to wear a pad when you do this.

3. Being constipated can sometimes cause yeast infections. You've gotta get regular. Eat apples, prunes, or figs. Drink lots of water and exercise.

4. Apple cider vinegar douches are very potent. They help establish the proper pH in your vagina. Once a day, add 1 tablespoon of vinegar to 1 quart of water, pour it in your douche kit (available at drugstores), lie down in the tub, and go to it. This is really effective when used in combination with yogurt suppositories.

5. Didn't you know? Garlic suppositories are the latest rage. Unwrap a clove and insert it into your vagina at night. Take it out in the morning. *Note: If you're allergic to garlic, don't try this cure. Ouch.*

6. Drink unsweetened cranberry juice.

7. Boric acid suppositories sound

scary, but those in the know swear by them. Buy empty capsules (size 0) and boric acid powder (available at the pharmacy). Fill up a capsule and insert one deeply into your vagina each morning and evening for three to seven days. If you have chronic yeast infections, continue for two to four more weeks.

J.O.B. BLUES

mission:
**To land that dream job, or at least manage
the crappy one without going postal.**

In a fair world, the job market would be a happy place.
It would be one in which employers were tickled pink to find you, a wildly
talented employee, and would scramble to give you a fat salary and fatter
expense account in exchange for the privilege of seeing you five days a
week. And in that same fair world, unemployment would be a time for
lounging—not scrounging. But we all know the bitter truth: Sometimes
the job market is a scary place where employers turn a blind eye to your
finer creative talents and the sky-high salary they justify. And if you're
unemployed, instead of enjoying your time off from the nine-to-five
world, you'll actually spend it worrying about how far you can stretch
that last measly paycheck and feeling lonely because all of your friends
are at work. The solution? Find new jobless (whoops, freelance) friends
or . . . get a job.

How to Be a Job Huntress. If you're out of work, treat job hunting as a full-time job. (Unemployment is not the time for you to catch up on matinees.) Start working the phone by 9 A.M., break for lunch, then continue until 4 or 5 P.M. At the very least, this routine will keep you from feeling like a loser. *Tip: You're allowed one or two coffee breaks (15 minutes) during the day.*

Pounding the Pavement: Landing a Paycheck

* Figure out what you want to do. Don't know? Figure out what you like to do. Think about your skills, personality traits, and favorite hobbies. But contemplate what floats your boat and what you require from a job. A feeling of integrity? (Try working for a nonprofit.) Night hours? (Performance artist.) The opportunity to yell at people? (Movie producer or the stock exchange.) Whatever it is, brainstorm and write it all down. Then read it through, do some research, and make a list of your top five dream jobs.

* Create a short but sweet résumé. Bluffing is sometimes OK in person (like if you've never waited tables but know you could pull it off), but *never* do it on paper.

J.O.B. Blues Tip #2

How to Cold-Call. Speak clearly and politely, but be direct. Sound assertive and self-confident.

* Get a sharp, well-groomed job-hunting ensemble together. **Job-Hunting Fashion Don'ts:** Lace, cleavage, midriff-baring ensembles, chipped nail polish, heavily lacquered hair, stilettos (passé), Lycra dresses, chewing gum, heroin chic (so passé).

* Check the newspaper for jobs or cold-call companies. (This really works! See Tip #2.) Networking is the ultimate job-hunting strategy—once again, it's all about who you know. If you can get somebody to recommend you, it will make the difference between your résumé landing in Human Resources Wasteland (the best way *not* to get hired) and on your future boss's desk.

* Make a great impression on the interview. Research the job or company

before you go in so that you can talk about it coherently. ("So what does this company do again?" will not make a good impression.) Have a firm handshake. Stand up straight, sit up straighter. Don't fidget. Be sincere. Speak clearly. And always send a short thank-you note after the interview.

J.O.B. Blues Tip#3

Temping is an excellent shortcut to landing a permanent job in a place where you really want to work. Call and ask which temp agencies your target company uses most. Then set up an appointment with the agency. Bonus: Temps are rarely given much responsibility, so you can scope out the company while getting paid for it.

How to Survive a Bad Job
(see also: Boss from Hell)

1. Take walks at lunchtime. Exercise helps clear the head and relieves you of any homicidal tendencies you may have suddenly developed.
2. As much as you may want to, do not develop the self-destructive habit of complaining about coworkers. It always comes around to haunt you and always makes you look like a jerk, no matter how right you are. Instead, think of it as an opportunity to gather material for that book you plan to write about demented department heads someday.
3. Start looking for a new job. (Duh.) But be sneaky about it. You don't want word to leak out before you're ready to get out of Dodge.
4. Try to get laid off. That way you can collect unemployment while you job hunt.

Useful Things You Can Learn During a Really Bad Job

- How to laugh heartily at very bad jokes.
- How to make every compliment sound sincere.
- How to "borrow" office supplies.
- How to keep a straight face in any situation.
- How to fake interest in job topics while actually planning your weekend.

KICK ASS

mission:
To expect the unexpected, anticipate the worst,
and then kick its butt if necessary.

Thanks to the recent Hollywood habit of making TV shows and summer flicks that feature crime-fighting, ass-kicking heroines, the phrase "hit like a girl" now has an entirely different meaning. Even better, real-life babes are also learning the joys of a well-done takedown through self-defense classes and martial arts training. If only we could all open up that can of whup-ass like Buffy. Here's what we've figured out: Fighting isn't about "muscle"—it's about speed and power, aka economy of action. Any self-defense move should be well practiced, swiftly delivered, and fully committed to (with your whole body behind it).

Remember: There are no rules. Your only goal is to escape unharmed. So don't be afraid to scream, pinch, kick, bite, hit below the belt, and generally do whatever the hell you have to do to get away.

Basic Self-Defense Techniques

Here are just a few prime areas to hit, and how to do it:

THE EYES AND THROAT

Curl your thumb, pinkie, and ring finger to the palm of your hand, holding the index and middle finger rigid. Strike (like a spear) straight into the eye or about a half inch above the hollow of the throat. Tip: You can also use your thumb in place of the index and middle fingers.

THE NOSE

Spread the fingers of your hand wide and tighten your hand. On the palm-side of your larger knuckles, the area should feel very solid. With this area, strike the creep right smack in the center of the nose.

THE FAMILY JEWELS

It's an oldie but a goodie—when in doubt, go straight for the groin. Bring your knee upward with all your force. If you can, grab the attacker's hips and pull him into the strike. Tip: Think of your knees as a point, and drive that point home!

Using your foot, strike your attacker with your instep. Or kick straight up and strike with your shinbone.

Using your hand, swing it straight up into the groin.

Kick-Ass Tip #1

Being a chick gives you a fundamental advantage in a fight, because no one expects you to know how to defend yourself. So if you have a combo of some well-practiced moves (or even just one), you've got the **Surprise Factor** on your side. (As in, "Surprise! How does this feel in your man parts, creep?")

Your hand should be in a fist or open, as when you strike the nose.

THE KNEES

With all your force, drive your heel forward into the kneecap. Or strike the inside of his knee with the inside of your foot. This works best if you are standing in front of the attacker with your back to him.

If the attacker is beside you, strike hard on the inside of the knee, driving your heel sideways and downward. (You should practice this one if you want to execute it effectively.)

Note: *Maintaining your balance on knee strikes is difficult, so practice, practice, practice.*

Kick-Ass Tip #3
All trained fighters learn to fight from **a crouch**. Contrary to popular belief, looming over your opponent is a disadvantage. If you fight from a crouch, you have greater control over your movements and better balance.

Kick-Ass Tip #2
Sign up for a self-defense class with your posse (friends, mother, sisters). Make it a **group thing**. And remember: Just because you learn how to throw a punch doesn't mean you're compromising your girlyhood. On the contrary, only a real woman knows how to drop a punk when she has to. Watch ass-kicking movies for inspiration—we recommend anything with Michelle Yeoh (martial-arts expert extraordinaire) in it.

knees!

LADY LUCK

mission:

**To win a million dollars, buy a new wardrobe, and retire to St. Bart's—
or at least look fantastic while you lose your rent money.**

Crack the Casino Code

1. Before you make your spectacular entrance into the casino, decide how much money you're going to play with, and stick to it. (A good rule of thumb is about the price of a nice dinner.) Absolutely no visits to the ATM are allowed after you lose your original stake.

2. Never bet more than 10% of your stake. If you start chasing the cash you've lost, the odds of going broke are much higher. Only raise your bets when you're ahead.

3. Forgo the free drinks. The boozier you get, the more likely you are to throw that cash away.

4. Beware the fickle ways of Lady Luck—a slippery little wench who loves to skitter off in the middle of your winning streak. If you've won more than $100, and then lose more than $20, switch dealers. Or go eat something. Anything to get you away from the table where Lady L. has abandoned you.

Strategies

Every gambler has her own system, good luck charms, and superstitions. Unfortunately, the odds are always in the dealer's favor, but these "rules" will, at least statistically, improve your chances.

For stylin' inspiration, check out *Casino* for Sharon Stone's ultimate high-roller wardrobe.

BLACKJACK

After you've been dealt a hand, here are a few things you should remember.

Lady Luck Tip #1

To paraphrase femme fatale Vesper Lind in *Casino Royale*, behaving like a high roller occasionally is an excellent treat. (Not to mention a chance to bust out your skintight lavender jumpsuit with the plunging neckline and a big, faux, golden fur.) Just don't turn into a freak about it. Here's a hint: If you catch yourself alone on a bus to Atlantic City with the 70+ crowd, talking excitedly about that 35 bucks you won the last time, you're in trouble. Tell the bus driver to drop you at the next Gamblers Anonymous center, pronto.

STAND/HIT

The most basic thing to know is when to *Stand* (take no more cards) and when to *Take a Hit*. In general, you should always Stand on:
* Hard hands* of 17 and up.
* Hands of 12 through 16, if the dealer's face card is 2 through 6.
* Soft hands of 18 and up.

THE SPLIT

A *split* is an option you have when you've been dealt two of the same card, or a pair. If you receive two 10s, for example, you can turn them both face-up, and play two hands. It's an important strategy for a good blackjack player, but you should know when to do it. Here's a quick guideline.

Always Split when:
   * You get a pair of aces or 8s.
   * You have any pair and the dealer's face card is 2 through 6.

* A hard hand has no ace or has an ace that must be counted as 1.

Never Split when:

* * You have a pair of 4s, 5s, or 10s.

DOUBLE DOWN

Knowing how to *Double Down* is another important part of being a suave blackjack player. It means that you double your bet midway through the game.

* A soft hand has an ace that can be counted as 11 without going over 21.

Here's when you should Double Down:

* * On 11, unless the dealer shows an ace.
* * On 10, unless the dealer shows an ace or 10.
* * On 9, if the dealer shows 3 through 6.
* * On soft hands* of 13 through 18, if the dealer's face card is 4 through 6.

CRAPS

The unfortunately named game of craps can be complicated but it's also fun, fun, fun! Not only does it often provide the best odds, but it always seems to be where the party is on the floor. It's also an ideal game for those of us with a teensy exhibitionist streak, in that it offers the chance to throw dice dramatically in front of an audience of screaming strangers. *Note: Gambling + Audience = Fun.*

So even if you never understand the math-laden nuances of the game, you can learn enough of the basics to have a good time and even win a chip or two. This is a very busy game with many betting options, but here's the basic point:

Let's say you're the "shooter," or the player whose turn it is to roll the dice. You roll two normal, six-sided dice. This means the numbers you roll will add up to anything from 2 to 12. If you roll 7 or 11, you've won and the round is over. If you roll 2, 3, or 12, that's a Craps. Craps is bad. It means you've lost, or "crapped out" (we're serious!), and the round is over. If you roll any other number than the ones listed above (in other words, if you roll 4, 5, 6, 8, 9, or 10), that number becomes something called the Point.

Now your goal is to roll the dice and have them add up to the Point again. The trick is, if you roll a 7 before you roll the Point, you lose. So does anyone who was betting on you (so you'd better be careful about who's betting on you!). If you roll something that's neither 7 nor the point, you simply roll again until you roll either 7 or the Point. And if you roll the Point, you win. Yippee!

Here are the easiest bets to begin with:

* Pass line
* Don't pass
* Come
* Don't come (This one's fun to yell out, if nothing else.)
* "Place" bets on 6 or 8

On the first four bets, always back your bet with the "odds" bet (which increases your winnings should your number hit). Of course, this is only if you have extra money to place on the odds; otherwise, wait until you're ahead a little.

Avoid like the plague:
Long-shot and one-roll bets, like "hardway 4."

ROULETTE
Look glamorous sitting at the roulette table with these short and sweet tips.

Best Bets:
* "Outside" the numbers, or even-money bets (red or black; odd or even; high or low)
* If 0 or 00 comes up, you lose only half of these wagers. Other bets are lost in full.

Casino Style

For added fun, we find the casino setting an excellent place to try out a saucy undercover ensemble. C'mon, it's the opportunity you've always wanted to see the world through cat-eye glasses, or better yet, through fake eyelashes. Here are some of our favorite ways to visit the casino incognito (also see Undercover):

THE RETIREE. Find anything made of man-made fibers (polyester is, of course, the classic) and be sure it's tight-fitting. Carry a plastic cup full of coins, and eat with enthusiasm at the $4 all-you-can-eat buffet. Be sure to keep that Virginia Slim burning in your ashtray at all times.

THE ARM CANDY. Wear something tight (boobs a-popping), tease that hair up high, and break out the sparkly eye shadow. For added effect, find a short, balding man to complete costume.

THE CONVENTIONEER. Slap a name badge on your corporate-casual ensemble, talk boisterously to anyone who makes eye contact with you, slap people on the back for no apparent reason.

THE PLAYER. (Only recommended for trust-funders.) Play games where the stakes—and the bets—are high; keep a look of intense concentration at all times; say things like "Triple down-red on the five-end." Extra points for having Arm Candy of your own.

Employee
the boss
Let's talk- RAISE
Let's talk- COMPROMISE
record of your achievements
Be Realistic in Expectations

LET'S MAKE A DEAL

mission:
To get what you want out of every negotiation
without putting anyone in a headlock.

The ability to negotiate is essential to being a winner at the game of life. In fact, this particular skill could mean the difference between a glamorous Gucci life ("Oh well, I'll just take both pairs") and a bargain-basement one ("Oh well, those puke-green ones are on sale, even if they do make my feet look like gunboats"). It can also help you in other areas of your life, like settling a tiff among the troops, pulling a fast one on your parents, or sweet-talking your significant other into buying you that fabulous lavender-and-hot-pink suede-and-python handbag.

The How-To

Valerie wants a raise. She has a job that she likes—set-designing for TV shows—but knows she should be paid more. Valerie knows her boss (let's call her Ms. Tightwad) doesn't want to give her any more money. How should she proceed?

1. BE PREPARED.

Valerie finds out everything she can about her field—most importantly, what other set designers get paid. She also checks out her competition and deduces that she is the best of the bunch at her workplace (naturally). She tries to anticipate what Ms. Tightwad might say to her, so she'll be ready for anything.

2. DECIDE WHAT YOU WANT, NEED, AND ARE WILLING TO SETTLE FOR.

Valerie decides that in order to survive in New York, she has to make at least $70,000 a year. She decides to shoot for the moon and ask for $90,000, figuring that Ms. Tightwad will try to lower that figure. Valerie also decides she's willing to go as low as $80,000. (That's a realistic target, since most of the people in her field make around that amount.)

Let's Make a Deal Tip #1:
Fridays Off. What if Ms. Tightwad's department really is financially strapped and a raise is out of the question? Your talks are at a standstill, and you've both decided to think on it for a day. If she's standing firm, be ready with your potential trade-offs *Note: This strategy should be used only after all other steps have failed.*

1. You only want to work four days a week. (Use the extra day for freelance that can supplement your income.)
2. You'd like to work from home.
3. You'd like to bring your dog in.
4. You'd like the use of a company car or a company cell phone.

This is your chance to use your imagination—how else can your company compensate you without taking money out of their budget?

3. CATCH THE BOSS IN A GOOD MOOD.

Valerie makes sure she asks Ms. Tightwad if they can meet at a time that works for both of them. Valerie knows that TW is a total freak on Fridays, since she has to review budgets. So Friday is definitely out.

4. ALWAYS NEGOTIATE IN PERSON.

Ms. Tightwad asks if they can talk on a day when she's out of the office. Valerie says no, because she knows that in person, she can read TW's body language and look around her office for visual cues for small talk. For example, TW has posters in her office of horses, and—guess what?—Valerie used to ride horses when she was a teenager.

5. NEVER NEGOTIATE WITH STRANGERS.

Ms. Tightwad then asks Valerie if she would be willing to talk with her new assistant, Mr. Small, whom Valerie has never met. She says she will fill Small in on the situation. Valerie agrees, then scopes out Small's office in advance. He has a bookshelf filled with books about WWII. Valerie's Great-uncle Pete just happened to be a highly decorated fighter pilot in WWII, and this is when all those longwinded family stories finally pay off. Our girl now knows she has something to get conversation flowing between her and Small.

6. ALWAYS LET THE NEGOTIATOR BRING UP THE SUBJECT AT HAND.

Valerie meets Mr. Small, they talk fighter pilots (*Thanks, Uncle Pete!*), then Valerie waits for him to bring up why she's there. She figures that she'll look too eager if she rushes into asking for more bucks. Soon, Small brings up the raise.

Let's Make a Deal Tip #2:
What Are You Really Worth? When evaluating your worth in the workplace on a comparative scale, consider your total contribution. Have you been there so long that it would take two people to make up for your experience? Or are your contacts so good that you save the company money on projects? Always calculate what it would cost to replace you—that's what your boss is doing during your negotiation.

Let's Make a Deal Tip #3:

Big Girls Don't Cry. Or beg, or whine, or throw tantrums. One card a savvy career girl never throws is the pity card. Pity is . . . well . . . pitiful. We know it's tempting to tell your boss that your car is in the shop, you're now officially on American Express's Most Wanted list, and that you're tired of telling people that you like your apartment cold. Don't do it. It'll only make your boss uncomfortable. He might throw you a bone, but your value to him will never be the same. You want your boss to know that you're an asset—he's lucky to have you around—not a burden he has to support.

7. FIGURE OUT THE NEGOTIATOR'S POSITION BEFORE YOUR OWN.

Valerie waits for Mr. Small to finish telling her why he thinks she should be happy with the money she gets. He lists all the benefits of working for the company (free pizza on Wednesdays, casual day on Fridays!). Valerie does not laugh out loud. Instead, she listens attentively while he explains why greasy takeout is, in fact, better than an extra ten grand a year.

8. KEEP A RECORD OF YOUR ACHIEVEMENTS.

Since Valerie was prepared, she has a list of reasons why she deserves that raise.

Valerie wraps it up by saying that she likes working there. The company is successful, her hard work has helped to contribute to that success, and it's important to her to work somewhere where she feels truly appreciated.

Valerie's List

* I came up with a shortcut this year that saved the company two days in setup time. I figure that saved the company roughly $20,000 a project.
* When Steve, aka Steve the Stoner, got fired earlier this year for sniffing the paint thinner, I took up the slack. I know for a fact that my "being a trouper" saved the company a cool $50,000 in Steve's salary.
* I make about $8,000 less than the going rate. I deserve that, and more.

9. KNOW WHEN TO SAY YES.

Finally, Valerie tells Mr. Small the salary she wants. In a cool, calm, and collected voice, she says, "I want $90,000 a year." When Small gasps, Valerie doesn't flinch—she knows it's part of the game. He tells her he couldn't possibly—how about $77,000? Now she's got him negotiating. She counters with $85,000. He pretends to think it over, pretends to be anguished, pretends to look at his budget, and finally offers her $82,000. She accepts and they shake hands. Valerie makes a charming joke to offset any negotiating tension and walks away happy. Mission accomplished!

MOBILIZATION

mission:
To keep your ride on the road and out of the shop.

Since the most highly trained Operative is prepared for any sticky situation, it's important to know what to do when your car has a meltdown. Let's face it, it's a major drag when your car dies, won't start, or you just don't have time (or the outfit) to change your flat. The easiest thing to do? Get a AAA membership.

But for those can-do chicas out there, learning how to change your oil, replace a tire, and jump-start your car gives you sweet liberation from overpriced mechanics. Think of it as a flip of the bird to all of those grease-covered jerks who've bilked you over the years.

Set yourself free, save 40 bucks, and learn how to:

Change Your Oil
Car manufacturers recommend that you change your oil every 3,000 to 6,000 miles (or every three months).

WHAT YOU NEED:

* Old clothes (we're not talking last season's dress) and rags
* The manual for your make of car (not all cars are alike)
* An oil filter wrench
* A crescent wrench
* Motor oil (ask a gas station attendant how many quarts your car requires)
* Oil filter
* Drip pan
* Small funnel

Mobilization Tip #1

DO NOT dump your oil in the sewer, or anywhere else for that matter. The high levels of lead will contaminate drinking water and kill wildlife. (You don't want the deaths of harmless little critters on your conscience, do you?) Instead, take it to a service station or auto supply store where they will recycle it.

HOW TO DO IT:

1. Park your car on a flat surface (set the emergency brake), and run it for a few minutes. Oil drains better when it's warm, but make sure you don't run it for too long—unless you're a masochist who's into hot oil burns.

2. Take the crescent wrench and shallow pan and crawl under the car. Find the oil plug under the engine block—it's on the underside of the oil pan.

3. Place the pan under the plug and unscrew it (counterclockwise) with the crescent wrench. Try to keep your arm raised so that oil doesn't run down it.

4. Watch the old oil rush out. *Note: The plug may fall into the pan along with the oil—don't worry.*

5. When all the oil has drained into the pan, screw the plug back in. Tighten it firmly, but don't strip the threads.

6. From above or below your car (depending on the make), find the oil filter and wrap the oil filter wrench around it. Unscrew the oil filter carefully, since it's full of (what else?) oil, and empty it in the drip pan.

7. Dip your fingertip into the new quart of oil, and lube the circular edge of the new filter (where it touches the metal engine surface).

8. Screw the new filter in with your hand, and tighten it firmly without overtightening.

9. Open your oil cap, which is situated on top of your engine (usually in plain view), drop the funnel in, and pour in the new oil. Replace the oil cap, and wipe up any oil drips on the engine.

10. Revel in your newly discovered inner Grease Monkey.

Change Your Tire
WHAT YOU NEED:
* A jack
* A properly inflated spare tire
* Lug wrench (with sockets that fit your wheel)
* Flashlight (because you know this will happen at night, for maximum inconvenience)
* Gloves and a tarp or small blanket (to keep your hands and knees from getting dirty)

HOW TO DO IT:
1. Make sure you're in a safe place (i.e., out of the way of traffic, not on a hill or incline). Put your hazard lights and emergency brake on.

2. Loosen the lug nuts on the tire you're changing. Sometimes they're hidden under the hubcap, sometimes not. Use your lug wrench or jack handle to pry the hubcap off if necessary, then turn each nut counterclockwise with your wrench. *Note: Leave the lug nut on the threaded shaft.*

3. Position the jack on a solid foundation, and raise it so that it just touches the car. Once you've got it in place, continue raising the car until there's enough room for you to slide the flat tire off.

4. Remove the lug nuts by hand, and pull the flat tire off.

5. Slide the spare into place, and tighten the lug nuts in opposite pairs so the wheel is firmly mounted.

6. Release the jack so the car is back on the ground, then tighten the lug nuts securely. Remove the jack.

7. Drive to a garage. The spare is not designed to last long (or to go at high speeds, so keep it nice and easy).

Jump-start Your Car

WHAT YOU NEED:

* A set of jumper cables—100% copper, heavy (4 to 8) gauge, and at least 10 feet long
* Old toothbrush or wire brush
* A car that's running

HOW TO DO IT:

1. Make sure both cars are turned off and parked side by side or facing hood to hood.

2. If there is white, green, or yellow corrosion around the terminals, clean it off with the wire brush.

3. Attach the positive cable end (red handle) to the positive terminal on the dead battery; then attach the other positive cable end to the battery in the car you're getting the jump from.

4. Attach the negative cable end (black handle) to the negative terminal on the battery in the running car, then attach the other negative cable end to the engine block or frame (an unpainted metal surface away from the battery) of the car with the dead battery.

5. Start the car that's providing the jump start.

6. Start your car. If your car doesn't immediately start, let the other car run for about five minutes, then try to start your car again.

7. Once your car is running, remove the cables starting in reverse (first the cable clamp attached to your car frame, then the negative cable clamp attached to the battery in the starting car, then the positive cable clamp on that battery, and finally, the positive clamp on your battery).

8. Thank the person who helped you, then drive your car for a while to make sure the battery is fully charged.

MORNING AFTER

mission:
To recover from a boogie night, pronto.

Too many martinis—shaken, not stirred—can make for a scary morning after. Mr. HotPants from the karaoke bar doesn't look so sparkly in the harsh A.M., does he? On top of this minor complication, you're also struggling with a hangover that could stop a hollow-tipped bullet. It happens to the best of us. Unfortunately, life's missions wait for no one, so you'd better find a fix, and fast.

There's no feel-better-quick cure for the pounding head, nausea, dry mouth, and other nonstop fun that come with a hangover. But there are a few things you can do to minimize the effects of a first-class bender.

1. Before you pass out—uh . . . *fall asleep*—down as much water or Gatorade as you can guzzle. It'll keep you from getting dehydrated. Also, pop a multivitamin that has minerals—it'll help your poor, mistreated body process all that alcohol.

2. Don't mix your alcohol.

A Little Story About Mixing Your Liquor

Lola goes out to meet some friends after work at Le Bar, where she downs a couple of **tequila** (to-kill-ya) gimlets. They decide to have dinner, and our gal has a couple of glasses of **red wine** with her meal. (A little wine doesn't count, does it?) After eating, the troops decide that the night is still young, so they move the party to another bar, where an already drunk Lola has a couple of **beers**. See Lola having fun. See Lola crawl up the stairs to her apartment. See Lola praying to the porcelain god, Ralph. See Lola wake up feeling like someone smacked her over the head with a two-by-four. Point made? We thought so.

Morning After Tip #1

Sugary drinks (anything made with liqueurs) will hit you harder the morning after. Too much sugar in the stomach mixes with the alcohol and makes for one sick party girl.

3. Post-hangover food theories abound. Eating bananas the morning after helps some recover. Others say eating tomato sauce (say, with spaghetti or lasagna) does the trick. Still others claim that a big greasy meal, like Mexican food or fast food, is the way to go. One thing's for sure: Eating before you go to sleep helps the most.

4. Caffeine comes in many forms—tea, coffee, soda, to name a few—and may make you feel better.

5. One more time: Eating while drinking is a smart (and yummy) way to lessen the effects of alcohol.

6. Take a bath to sweat out the toxins.

7. Do like the French, and down a glass of water after every alcoholic drink.

8. The best way to prevent a hangover? Don't drink too much, you putz.

Around-the-World Cures

It's been said that Russian women who've downed too much vodka the night before drink fizzy cabbage juice for hangovers. In Germany, some say marinated fish is great for the morning after. The Chinese sip kudzu tea to help them sober up. Mexican partiers swear by menudo, a soup made from tripe and hominy.

Morning After Tip #2

Some studies say that taking aspirin, acetaminophen, or ibuprofen while you've been drinking can be hazardous to your health. Painkillers are metabolized through the liver, and we all know what alcohol does to a person's liver, don't we? Use your own judgment.

Some say **"hair of the dog"** (drinking more alcohol) is the best way to get over a hangover. Actually, it's a good way to guarantee that you'll become an alcoholic.

PEE STANDING UP

mission:
To answer nature's call while on the go.

It's a cruel world, and it's even crueler when you've just downed a gallon of H_2O and there's not a ladies' room in sight. Sadly, some businesses deny customers the right to use their bathrooms. Frankly, we think such stinginess should be outlawed, and all restroom keys should be liberated for the people. But hey, we're not in charge of the Ladies' Room Laws, and unfortunately, neither are you. That means it's your job to convince the Keepers of the Key that you are a risk they should be willing to take. Here's a list of our favorite tactics:

1. THE MEDICAL ALERT
Buy one of those medical bracelets they sell at drugstores. Keep it in your car for emergencies like these. Calmly tell the employee that you have a serious medical condition that could be aggravated if you don't use the bathroom immediately, and show them your wrist (which is now clad in said

bracelet). If they still don't budge, ask for their card and threaten them with a lawsuit. It probably won't work but it'll at least be satisfying.

2. THE PREGNANCY PLOY
Play the sympathy card and tell them you're pregnant.

For the Truly Desperate

The worse the neighborhood, the longer you'll have to hold it since businesses in these areas are less likely to let you use their rest rooms. So hang on until you get to a safer area.

It's kind of scary in a survivalist sort of way, but you could always carry around an empty glass jar in your car for this particular emergency. *Note: For the sake of your next passenger, you must empty and wash it when you're done. Otherwise, you could seriously scar a friendship.*

What Every Girl Should Know—How to Pee Standing Up

Let's face it, who wants to squat over a gas station toilet anyway, praying your legs don't give out and smack you down on a skanky toilet? Buy a Freshette or TravelMate, and keep it in your car's Bug-Out Bag (see Hit the Road). These nifty gadgets enable you to go standing up, without even pulling your pants down. Alternatively, learn to pee standing up—who knew? *Note: Practice makes perfect, so hit the shower for some pretend emergencies.*

Here's the drill:
1. Clean your hands with soap and water or a towelette.
2. Pull your pants down a few inches or hike your skirt up and move

your panties away from the crotch. Pee stains on your outfit are no fun.

3. Make a V with your pointer finger and your middle finger, and, well, spread yourself. Spread the inner lips of your vagina (labia minora, FYI) with your V.

4. Lift (this is key) and pee. *Note: You run the risk of dribbling if you don't follow this step perfectly.*

5. Wipe yourself off. Adjust your clothing, wash your hands, and strut out like the bad Mama Jama you are.

Most chain restaurants and hotel lobbies have rest rooms that the public can use.

Nature's Call Tip #1
The "Lose the Dude." If you're with a male friend, leave him outside and ask to use the rest room solo. The business owner may be less likely to let a couple use the bathroom. Besides, have you ever seen a dude who had trouble finding a place to pee?

PINK SLIP

mission:

Getting the ax—and bringing it down—with no blood and a minimum of tears.
Bonus points for successful office-supply raid on way out of building.

Getting the Ax

If you're a girl with a wide streak of the nonconformist (our favorite streak), chances are you'll find yourself on the business end of a pink slip one day. It's not that you're a failure; it's just that you couldn't bring yourself to say "Super Size" with the perkiness your drive-thru manager expected. Time to move on, and no need to torture yourself over it. In fact, you're in fine company (with heads of state, rock stars, and, yes, even the author of this book). Instead of feeling like a loser, try to see the sunny side: This could be the change you've been needing.

Give yourself a few days to indulge in the Just-Been-Fired Blues (complaining to friends over a margarita or two never hurts), but then move on to finding a new paycheck. (See "J.O.B Blues.") If your former job involved a skanky boss (see "Boss from Hell"), begin your tell-all memoir to exact revenge.

GOOD THINGS ABOUT GETTING FIRED

* Now you can move on to your dream job.
* Now you can reassess your life—hey, no nine-to-five to keep you from moving to another state.
* Best of all, now you can collect unemployment. (Although you won't be living high on the hog, trust me.)

The Turnaround: Giving the Ax

Handing out a pink slip is never easy. Even the most hard-boiled operative has a heart and hates to see a grown-up cry. But a job is a job and if someone's not up to snuff, you have to give him or her the heave-ho. Think of it this way: If someone's consistently not pulling his weight, chances are everyone else is working overtime to pull it for him. It's your obligation to fix the problem.

Of course, there's a wrong way and a right way to go about ditching someone. Here's a primer.

THE SETUP

When he started, Dick seemed like the perfect receptionist: well-mannered, energetic, and eager to please. But lately, Dick has become the employee from hell. He leaves the office for hours without telling anyone, makes spectacular mistakes when copying reports, and usually gives you completely illegible phone messages. You've warned Dick that his job performance, well, sucks and have

The Hiring 1-2-3s: Stop, Look, and Listen

The next time you have a position to fill, don't talk too much during the job interview. Instead, explain the job's requirements and spend the rest of the time letting your potential employee talk about his or her last job and boss, her skills and experience, etc. Really listen to what's being said. That way you'll get a better handle on who it is you're hiring. You may even learn how to stop hiring loser employees like Dick.

given him time to clean up his act. (The last phone message he gave you had six digits.) You've documented your complaints and are being reasonable with your expectations. ("Seven digits at least, Dick. Please.") But Dick's performance hasn't changed, and he's clearly not taking the job or your warning seriously. Check your employee handbook and federal laws to make sure you're within your rights to give Dick the old boot.

Do's and Don'ts for Letting Someone Go

Do:
* Speak honestly and very clearly about the reasons for the discharge. ("Did you really have to high-five the CEO?")
* Ask someone else to sit in (preferably a member of Human Resources) as support for Dick.
* Explain any severance packages, benefits that continue, or job placement counseling in clear and concise terms.
* Have at hand a list of company property (keys, Xerox card, etc.) that Dick has to return. No one wants him coming back for last-minute supplies.

Don't:
* Get personal by saying things that could humiliate the guy. (For example, "Are you a total moron or just a slacker?")
* Give him any hope of a turnaround. It's counterproductive , and you've made your final decision. Tell him firmly that the purpose of the meeting is to let him go.
* Insist that he leave the building as soon as your talk is done. Instead, give him time to pack his personal effects and leave during a low-visibility period (after-hours or on a weekend).
* Sabotage the employee's chances of getting a job elsewhere. Discuss with him a "story" you will stick to when called as a reference.

SCAM CITY

mission:
To scam a good deal while staying on the right side of the law.

There are discounts available everywhere for the asking—but the point is, you have to ask. Perhaps you've never heard of the following hustles, or perhaps you know them like the back of your manicured hand. Here goes:

Hustles We Love

1. **The Kid's Fare.** Order movie tickets by phone and get the child's fare (usually half price). When you go to pick them up, the ticket taker rarely looks to see what type of ticket you have, so you get the movie at half price. If you get busted, act dumb. You may have to pay the higher fare—or the guy may actually be charmed by your act.

2. The Taste Tester. Score your Saturday tea at a superstore or market that specializes in "free taste setups." You can make a meal out of their samples and do your shopping. *Note: We like the mini quiches.*

3. The Press Pass. Scoring this is like having the Super Gold Pass to the entertainment world. It's also the ulti-mate in scammer accessories. If you have to work for it, *c'est la vie. Note: An alternative to a press pass is to start a band, magazine, or become a club promoter or DJ. These are more valid ways to get the key to the city.*

Taste Tester

4. The Happy Return. The golden rule of drag queens and stylists alike: Buy clothes, wear them once, and return them. Your wardrobe will be drop-dead fabulous, and your bank account will breathe a sigh of relief. Make sure you don't remove the tags. (Tuck them in where they're not visible.) Do not get pit stains (or any other kind of stain) on the clothes, and make sure they don't stink after you wear them. *Note: This hustle is not recommended if you tend to get too attached to your clothes to return them.*

5. The Seat Saver. If there's a long line at the movie theater, have your friends wait in line, then go up to the ticket seller and buy tickets for every-one. Go back to your friends, and give them their tickets. While they wait, go up to the front of the line, and find some unsuspecting guy. Give him your most stunning smile, and ask if you can join him.

Once you're in the theater, save seats for you and your friends (it helps if you have coats or a newspaper). This way, everyone can sit together. *Note: This also works if you're solo and just don't feel like waiting in line.*

Scam City Tip #1

Ask and Ye Shall Receive. Ask for discounts everywhere. One shrewd subject we know tried this as an experiment. For an entire week, every time she paid for something, she asked if she could get it, well, cheaper. She explained that she was a good customer who had been frequenting the place for a while. Amazingly enough, it worked. She scored discounts and deals in places she never expected—from the phone company (free minutes for 6 months) to the dry cleaners. Try this and see if it works for you. *Note: The main reason this strategy works is that companies don't want you to leave them for their competitor. So if you're dealing with a corporation—say, a phone company that offers long distance—explain that you think your bill is too high and that the competitor is offering better rates. Then wait to see if they start dealing. Play hardball and don't take no for an answer.*

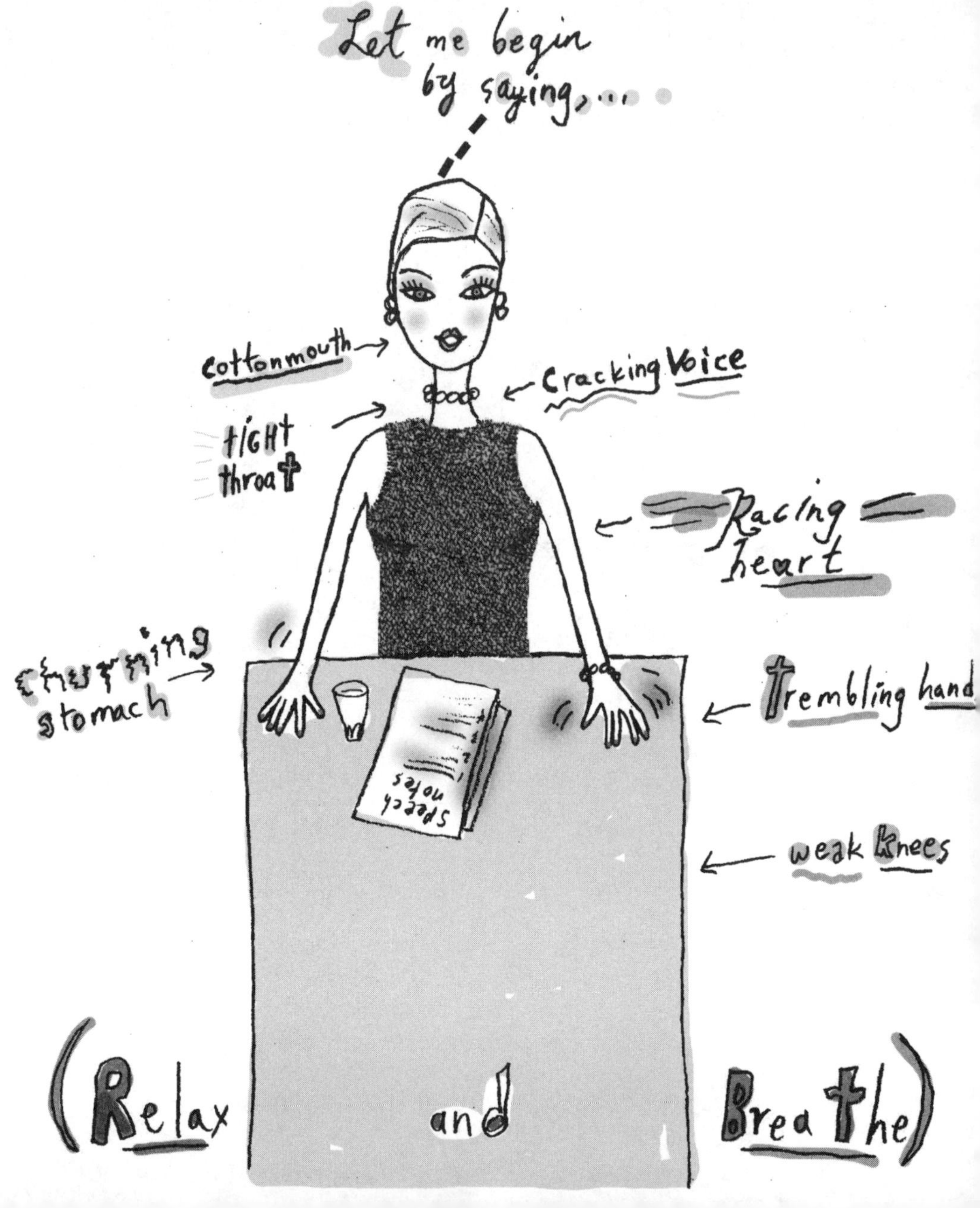

Let me begin by saying, . . .
cottonmouth
Cracking Voice
tight throat
Racing heart
churning stomach
trembling hand
speech notes
weak knees
(Relax and Breathe)

SCHMOOZING, SOCIALIZING, AND SURVIVING THE SPOTLIGHT

mission:

To work a room, a Rolodex, or your dad's bowling club until someone gives you your damn dream job.

Every job huntress should know how to schmooze, even if she works the counter at McDonald's—wait, make that *especially* if she works the counter at McDonald's.

If you are a successful schmoozer, you will expand not only your circle of acquaintances but also the number of groovy opportunities that life presents you. If you are a bad schmoozer, you will come across as a big fake, which only makes people feel creepy.

There are no Top Secret Tricks to being an effective networker—just six simple rules.

1. **Have a firm handshake.** Nothing gives a worse first impression than a wet-noodle grasp.

2. **Be subtle.** When introducing yourself to Big Bill, don't blurt out that you've been trying to land a job at his company. Take your time, and be sincere.

3. **Overcome your shyness.** Everyone is nervous about meeting new people—learn to power through your jitters. It helps to be direct: "Hi, my name is Ruby, and I wanted to introduce myself." Realize that even the most successful person can be a little timid when it comes to meeting new people.

4. **Find common ground.** Take a cue from your surroundings. In a bookstore, talk books and writers; in a gallery, talk art or people-watching; at a football game, talk sports or athletes; at a dinner, talk restaurants or food.

5. **Be tactful.** If you're talking to the head of BigAss Records, don't ask her out for a cup of coffee or tell her your little sister is in a band. (Believe me, she doesn't have the time and hears the band pitch from roughly half the people she meets.)

6. **Keep it real.** Nothing is worse than talking to a scary phony. Remember, you're trying to build contacts for life, so let the real you come through.

Great Ways to Network

* Cold-call (you'd be surprised how well this works)
* Volunteer (at clubs, committees, neighborhood meetings, conferences, environmental groups, shelters)
* Intern (at a magazine, film, or record company, or any other business you're interested in)
* E-mail (many companies list their employees' e-mail addresses online)

Survive the Spotlight

If you're a successful schmoozer, more than likely you'll climb ever higher on the career ladder. And when you reach an appropriately dizzying height, it will happen: you'll be asked to speak in public. Yes, there will come a time when you'll be forced to address an audience—and you will survive.

THE SYMPTOMS

Churning stomach, nausea, sweating, using the bathroom a lot, hyperventilating, racing heart, weak knees, cottonmouth, cracking voice, vomiting, trembling hands, tight throat. Sound fun so far?

THE CURE

* Take deep, slow, relaxing breaths from your stomach.

* Realize the experience isn't as terrifying as you think. Instead of imagining the worst thing that could happen, think of the best. (And so what if the worst thing does happen? It only makes for a better story to tell your friends.)

* Relax your throat by yawning.

* Make eye contact with the foreheads or hairlines of your audience (sometimes eyes can be too distracting). *Note: For some speakers, it helps to make eye contact. Once you're more experienced, you'll find that it helps to engage your audience and forget about yourself.*

* Perform more often. The more you do it, the better you feel.

* Don't mistake adrenaline for fear.

{Jane Bond pad}

← bamboo

← thrift store glass w/ apple martini

← Foreign maps

Paris

{Mata hari pad}

← peacock feather

lacquer furniture

Decat su casa

{Cleopatra's pad}

← Columns w/ cherubs

Rose Oil

← for the tub

mirrors mucho

{emma peel pad}

faux Zebra rug

bowler hat →

STYLE PILE MAKEOVER

mission:

To breathe some worldly life into your deadbeat digs.

You think of your home as your shelter—a refuge where you can escape from weird bosses and annoying friends into your own singular space. Still, you also want it to be a place where you can entertain comfortably, whether it's several people or that one special guest.

Here are a few themes inspired by our favorite stylin' heroines that we think make for supreme swankiness.

Survivalista Styles That Inspire

We've collected a few tricks to ensure that your shelter is *trés* chic. Just remember: A shelter should delight, not bite.

JANE BOND'S BACHELOR PAD

Never heard of James's half sister? That's because she kept a lower profile than her flashy brother—proving she was the better Double Agent after all.

THREE DECOR TIPS

* Pick two primary colors, such as yellow and red, and use them as inspiration for your space. Paint the walls yellow and make red slipcovers for your furniture, accenting the room with eggplant-colored throw pillows, glasses, vases, or picture frames.

* Find an old vanity, display case, or vintage bar, and make it the centerpiece of the living room. Customize it with paint, fringe, framed photos, and a vase filled with flowers. Keep it stocked with your favorite liquor, teas, Japanese crackers, cashews, spicy olives, and a collection of funky thrift-store drinking glasses.

* To give your shelter that worldly *je ne sais quoi*, hang bamboo curtains in the windows and old city maps of Paris, London, and Berlin on the walls.

ESSENTIAL GADGET: camera-watch for recording all visitors to your shelter. Extra Survivalista points if visitors are unaware of documentation.

SCENT TIP: When contemplating your next operation, use Stay Focused* in a water diffuser to enhance your thoughts.

DRINK OF CHOICE: apple martini

SUGGESTED COLORS: black, dark red, green, eggplant, and yellow

*Stay Focused: Combine 5 drops of pure, essential clary sage oil, 5 drops basil oil, 5 drops lavender oil, and 2 drops geranium oil with water in the diffuser's bowl.

MATA HARI'S MYSTERIOUS LAIR

Mata Hari was an ineffective Double Agent in most respects, except when it came to style.

THREE DECOR TIPS

* Buy inexpensive small blue-and-white Chinese vases (from Pier 1, Cost Plus, Chinatown) and fill them with peacock feathers (available at any crafts store), sticks, fresh herbs, dried flowers, or inexpensive red carnations. Place them in groupings around your shelter, along with ferns (or other houseplants with pretty leaves) placed in larger Chinese and terra-cotta pots.

* Buy sari fabric or chinoiserie (shiny Chinese fabric embroidered with flowers, birds, etc.), and use it for curtains, pillows (you should have lots of huge pillows on your bed or sofa for that ultraseductive, exotic mood), or bedspreads. Also, get a white shag rug for your floor and faux leopard or tiger fur to drape over the bed, sofa, or chairs.

* Lacquer your dressers, tables, and chairs in red and black, and change any hardware to Asian-themed knobs and pulls.

*In the Mood:
Combine 10 drops each of jasmine, rose, and ylang ylang oil in a 2-ounce dark glass bottle with spray top. Add 2 ounces of water and shake well before spraying.

ESSENTIAL GADGET: voice-disguising telephone for that weekly call to your favorite deliverin' drugstore for condoms, cake, and cosmetics

SCENT TIP: Spray In the Mood* in the air when you're feeling frisky—alone or with company.

DRINK OF CHOICE: sex on the beach

SUGGESTED COLORS: turquoise, crimson red, gold, ebony, and pale orange

CLEOPATRA'S CASA D'AMOUR

Cleopatra didn't just decorate a room—she conquered it (just like she did a certain Roman emperor).

THREE DECOR TIPS

* Hang sheer fabric or mosquito netting above your bed (decked with white Egyptian cotton sheets and white satin pillows) to create a veiled effect. A saucy picture—preferably on black velvet—of an amorous couple looks particularly fine hanging above the bed. Keep the lighting seductive with bedside lamps and candles.

* Turn your bathroom into an alluring grotto with potted palms on columns, plaster statues of cherubs or naked women, dim lighting, gold towels, and a satiny shower curtain. If you can, epoxy glass beads in purple, black, and gold

along the rim of your tub to create a spilling-over effect.
* Mirrors, mirrors, mirrors—in the kitchen, living room, and especially the bedroom.

ESSENTIAL GADGET: the Clapper, for instant mood lighting. (Your date won't have a chance.)

SCENT TIP: Cleopatra's famous seduction of Mark Antony began when she scented the sails of her ship with rose oil. Try Queen Bee* in the tub to feel like you rule.

DRINK OF CHOICE: cream and Amaretto

SUGGESTED COLORS: purple, black, gold, milky white, and rose

*Queen Bee:
Put 5 drops each of pure, essential oils (such as sandalwood, ylang ylang, and patchouli) in a full tub of water, and mix well with your hand before getting in.

PATTY HEARST'S PREPPY HIDEAWAY

First she was a deb, then a revolutionary. This is Survivalista home decor—Symbionese Liberation Army-style.

THREE DECOR TIPS

* Paint your walls lilac, the trim (molding, windows, baseboard) in shell pink, and hang photos of female style icons (like old-school actress Ava Gardner, diva Mary J. Blige, or writer Colette) in cheap frames you've painted chocolate brown.
* Hang window curtains in pink camouflage trimmed with green ribbon.
* Alternate your use of colors (pink kitchen cupboards, green knobs, brown bedspread, pink pillows, green lamp shades) throughout your shelter.

ESSENTIAL GADGET: caller ID to determine identity of potential admirers, stalkers, and/or credit card company employees (See Beat the Bank)

SCENT TIP: Feeling overly suspicious? Massage Born Yesterday* into your temples and body.

DRINK OF CHOICE: surfer on acid (Malibu rum, Jaegermeister, pineapple juice,

grenadine—chilled and served as a shot)
SUGGESTED COLORS: army green, shell pink, camel, lilac, and chocolate brown

*Born Yesterday: Blend 4 ounces almond oil with 15 drops each of lavender and jasmine oil.

EMMA PEEL'S MOD LODGE

Independent and chic, she Avenged bad style every-where.

THREE DECOR TIPS

* Paint your living room white with black trim, and hang black-and-white polka-dotted curtains in your living room windows.
* Keep the room looking minimal with white slip-covered furniture (with pink-and-black polka-dotted pillows), a faux zebra-skin rug, and thrift-store tables that you've stripped and stained white.
* Hang framed posters of '60s British films on the walls. Add a hat rack, and hang one bowler and one umbrella on it.

ESSENTIAL GADGET: the Fogmaster for instant Jolly-Old atmosphere

SCENT TIP: After a busy day of subversive activity, clear your mind at night with Thoughts Be-Gone.*

*Thoughts Be-Gone: In 1/2 cup of warm water add 6 to 8 drops of eucalyptus oil. Place by your bed when you're ready to sleep.

DRINK OF CHOICE: lemon drop, because you gotta love the Peel

SUGGESTED COLORS: black, white, pink, gray, and green

SWEET REVENGE

mission:

To feel the joy of payback without becoming creepier than your target.

Ever been dumped? Had someone spread lies about you? (Even worse, had them spread the true stuff?) Maybe you didn't get that promotion because your coworker took credit for your hard work? If you answered yes to any of the above questions, then you have probably been pissed off enough to crave the bittersweet taste of revenge.

We'd love to give you a no-nonsense list of ways to extract revenge— a really great car-keying, phone-tampering, new-girlfriend-stalking list— but we won't. Thing is, hurting other people is dumb. Worse, it's not that satisfying. So even though you think your boyfriend's car windows deserve to be smashed, heaving that brick will only brand you a psycho and him as the victim. Of course, the desire to disfigure his car is totally natural (and, in fact, can make for excellent fantasy), but what you decide to do with that emotion is what makes you different from an animal. Meaning, that's what our brains are for: to stop and consider the consequences before we attack.

When you stoop to someone else's low standards, you're letting people know you're hurt—and desperate to be noticed: Jerk: 10, You: 0.

The lowdown: Revenge looks great on TV. In real life, it doesn't look or feel so good.

So what'll make you feel better?

How 'bout:

* Moving into a fabulous new apartment.
* Hanging with friends who believe what you say (and not what they hear).
* Becoming spectacularly successful at your job.
* Landing an Italian lover; and knowing that while you can move on and become a better person, that loser who hurt you will always be stuck in the muck of his own rottenness.

Groovy Revenge Thought for the Day

An eye for an eye only ends up making the whole world blind.—Mahatma Gandhi

Sweet Revenge Tip #1

Instead of sending that hate letter to the person who hurt your feelings, send it to your girlfriends so they can add their own slams. Or write it just for yourself and make a ritual out of burning it. Just the act should make you feel better.

Of course, none of this means you should just roll over. Letting people know you're hurt is really important, not to mention an excellent excuse for a martini-soaked blues-fest with your friends. But has anyone's mind ever been changed by an extreme act of revenge? Sorry, but no. Revenge is about you. And you, my friend, should move on.

The best form of revenge? Feeling and looking good. Just make sure the creep who hurt you hears (from you or your friends) about how fabulous you've become. It'll drive the jerk crazy. Now *that's* payback.

A Simple Spell

Before you head out to your local magick shop for a nasty little spell to cast, think twice. Wiccans* believe in something called the Threefold Law, which means that everything you do comes back to you three times worse. Like karma, it's about the energy you put out.

*another name for witches or anyone else who follows the nature-based, pagan religion

A-List Tactics
be a regular
call ahead
use a fake name
go on a slow night-mon., tues.
hello, I made a reservation
My name is Blaine Hilton.

TABLE FOR TWO

To hustle your way into the hottest feed spot in town without having to wait tables there.

Sure, we know that those of us with real style don't need to follow the herd to the latest quasi-fusion-bistro just to prove that we're in the know. Then again, sometimes you want to see what all the fuss is about. Sometimes you want to see if Tom Cruise really does eat there. And sometimes you just want to taste the damn pineapple-glazed cinnamon-infused pork chop for yourself.

Whatever the reason, you can bet that getting past that nasty little prig with the power complex and the reservations list will be a challenge. Luckily, we love a good challenge, especially those that involve a possible encounter with Tom Cruise and/or food (not necessarily in that order). Here's a list of some of our best haute cuisine strategies.

Tactical Maneuvers

1. Become a regular. You don't have to be Madonna to get the table you want. Maître d's and servers will go out of their way to make their best customers (read: most regular customers) comfortable.

2. Don't be a shrew. Rudeness (as in "I can get you fired!" or the hands-down favorite of maître d's everywhere: "Do you know who I am?!") will get you nowhere fast, whether you're complaining about not being able to get a reservation or griping about the wait. Call ahead and tell the reservations person you'd appreciate being put on the cancellation list. Call back to ask if anything has opened up. And be flexible—especially while you're building a relationship. If they offer you a six o'clock table, jump on it. You can always linger for a while as the glitterati come in.

3. Go on a slow night. Obviously, some restaurants are packed every night of the week, while others count Thursday through Sunday as their busy nights. Find out when their slowest night is and call ahead to get reservations for that evening.

Spread the Wealth

When all else fails and you absolutely have to get into Chez Fancy Fork, try a little old-fashioned palm greasing. Go to the restaurant even though you don't have a reservation. Be very discreet, and slip the maître d' a twenty (or a fifty, depending on how popular the restaurant is) while asking if there are any tables available for that night. You'll probably find yourself seated within minutes.

4. Give a fake last name. Hey, we're not above a white lie now and then when faced with a particularly stubborn situation. Just don't be too heavy-handed about it; stay away from the obvious surnames

like Rockefeller and Trump. A less well-known family name (whose members you just happen to slightly resemble) can be amazingly effective. Experiment and see which name works for you.

5. Get to know the maître d'. If you've gotten cozy with the person who seats people, you will find yourself getting a table faster than people who have been waiting longer than you. Fact: This works at the diner down the street, too.

When you do score that reservation, make sure you request the table you want, or at least rule out the one you don't want. Otherwise, you may find yourself seated in that lovely spot across from the toilets. Bummer.

The Flip Side of Reservations

If you're going to be late for—or entirely miss—your reservation, always call to let the restaurant know. A reservation is an unwritten contract. If they think they're getting a party of eight, they will buy extra food, and possibly even ask an extra server to come in. If you expect to be treated well, return the favor.

And if you arrive for your reservation on time and the table isn't ready, it's perfectly acceptable for the maître d' to ask you to wait in the bar. Waiting fifteen minutes is fine; longer than that and the restaurant should buy you a drink. After all, they're making extra money by overbooking their tables and having people buy $8 cocktails in their bar while they wait. Many restaurants do this automatically, but usually you have to say something and call it to their attention—nicely.

Tweedy + Leather *Trimmed*

sporty cheeky tote

sensible for

Job Interview

playful for 1rst Date (daytime)

UNDERCOVER

Think about it—where would Gwen Stefani be without her ever-changing fashion statements? India Arie without her 'do-wraps? Sure, they'd probably all be on top anyway, but it's their style that sets them apart. Clothes may not make the diva, but they can be a great shorthand for communicating their fabulousness. Fact: Sometimes you can judge a book by its miniskirt.

Thing is, you want to be sure you know the right shorthand for the right setting. Let's review a few classic situations, along with recommended style tips:

Situation: Meet the Parents

1. Leave the "hoochie" at home, and keep those boobs under wraps. You don't need to flaunt your sexual power over their offspring by wearing your skintight best.

2. No siren-red lipstick. You're better off with I'm-ready-to-bear-your-grandchildren pink.

3. The more conservative, the better. Don't go overboard with a Mormon routine, but be respectful and wear clothes that say, "I'm prepared to suck up as much as necessary."

A Big Fat Lie

As much as the corporate world would like you to believe that the interview process is about your personality, it isn't. So don't wear clothes that scream who you are. Unless, of course, you're really a mild-mannered, responsible job applicant. As if.

Situation: Job Interview

1. Tailor your dress to fit the workplace. What flies at your record label job (T-shirts, leather, vintage clothing) will bomb at an investment house. So keep your piercings to yourself.

2. Shine your shoes and keep jewelry to a minimum: a watch (to show you're timely), an understated necklace if you like, and a simple pair of small hoop or stud earrings. (Dangly earrings, for some reason, just scream "unreliable" in a job interview.)

3. A simple job interview uniform: A boat-neck shirt with 3/4 sleeves or a long-sleeved button-down shirt goes great with a pair of dress pants or a knee-length skirt. Top it all off with a little blazer. Tip: Fitted velvet blazers are great for instant style and won't frighten prospective employers. Find them at Loehmann's or other discount designer stores; if you're on the small side, shop the little boy's section at Goodwill. (The sleeves might be a little short, but that'll show off your watch.)

Situation: First Date

1. Don't put all the goods on display the first night. Instead, try to balance your masculine and feminine energies—that way you're prepared for whichever direction the date might turn (i.e., midnight make-out or escape at eight. See Ditch the Date).

2. Try this: red lipstick but no eye shadow; low-slung pants with high heels; a chamois-colored A-line leather skirt with a white T-shirt.

3. Do your nails, but don't go for the fancy manicure. That way if you don't like the guy, you won't feel like you worked too hard for nothing.

Situation: Wedding Day (Someone Else's!)

1. Check the invite for the time and location of the ceremony and reception. A garden party is more informal than a church ceremony. You can wear colors, prints, even black. Dresses are preferred, but a skirt and pretty top are fine, too. Leave the stilettos at home. Tip: Heels are hell at those lawn parties.

2. Don't compete with the wedding party or try to upstage the bride (no white!). If you're unsure of the dress code, feel free to dress up, but leave the plunging tops and microminis at home.

3. Now is your chance to wear a really big hat, which is, let's face it, an opportunity that doesn't present itself often enough in life.

Situation: Impress the Clients

1. A little style savvy is OK, but now is not the time to get trendy. Instead, your look should say, "You can trust me with your money, Honey."

2. Double-check the important details, like that your shirt is ironed, the creases in your pants are straight, your shirt collar is flat, there aren't any loose threads or buttons hanging, and your face is clear of any wandering mascara or runaway lipstick.

3. Make sure your shoes are in great shape. Scuffed or uneven heels, tired-looking leather, and cheap shoe materials are not signs of success.

VELVET ROPE

To boldly cross the line that turns you from a "one of them" into a "one of us."

Industry parties, new nightclubs, society weddings, and invite-only restaurant openings all present a sticky problem: How does a conniving chica get on the other side of the velvet rope? Barring sleeping with the person who does the door (one word: *skanky*), here's a little how-to that will whisk you from the D-list (Don't Come Back) to the A-list (Always Nice to See Ya).

Tactical Maneuvers

1. LOOK LIKE YOU BELONG

Nervous body language and stammering will get you nowhere fast. Self-confidence and self-possession will open doors. If you look like you need to get in, you probably won't.

2. ARRIVE IN STYLE

Don't pull up in your 1981 Toyota Tercel hatchback. Instead, take a cab (*trés chic*) or

DOOR GUY STRATEGY #1: THE WHAMMY

We know a New York club-hopper who uses this technique with a 75% success rate. As she approaches a club with a long line out front, she looks directly at the door guy (that's the Whammy). She maintains her look in an important and meaningful way ("We both know you should know who I am, so don't make me get you fired") as she walks purposefully toward the front of the line. To pull this off, imagine that you are Angelina Jolie (or whoever you pretend to be when you give your bathroom-mirror acceptance speech) while you stare him down. If he dares to stop you, the jig is probably up. To save face, tell him that your party is already inside and you just wanted to join them.

go with a friend who has an SUV (trés bad for the environment but looks money nonetheless). *Note: Showing up on foot looks like you couldn't afford a ride.*

3. GET TO KNOW THE POWERS THAT BE

We aren't suggesting that you should sleep your way into any party—a trashy and (frankly) amateurish ploy. No, a better alternative is to get to know the promoter. To get on the list, call the club that day or the night before, and ask to speak with the manager or promoter. Once you've got him on the phone, convince him of your fabulousness. If that doesn't work, next time call him and lie and convince him you're someone else. (See Door Guy Strategy #3; see also Tactical Maneuver #7 from Table for Two).

Velvet Rope Tip #1

The old guest list switcheroo is one of our favorite tricks. While you're out of sight, have your partner in crime hang out where the guest lists are kept until she sees a name on the list. When she does, she'll come tell you what it is. You approach the keepers of the list, give that name (guest lists always have a +1), and the two of you are in like Flynn. *Note: This trick always works better at small clubs; at larger venues, list keepers are more likely to ask for an ID.*

4. PROMOTE YOURSELF

Act like you work there. This may enable you to glide through the front door, but more likely than not, you'll have to stop, drop, and roll through a back entrance. Observe the staff's comings and goings and enter where they do. Be sure to watch out for security.

5. TRAVEL IN PACKS

A girl posse is much more appealing to a door guy than a gal flying solo or one who surrounds herself with a pack of guys. Promoters want females in their clubs, reasoning accurately that male clubgoers will then spend more money.

6. FIND A FRIEND

While waiting on the other side of the velvet rope, glance at your watch. Give a friendly acknowledgment to the gorillas manning the door, and let them know you're just waiting on a friend. Give yourself about 5 or 10 minutes, then look inside the party, and yell to someone inside, "There you are! I've been waiting out here." Then, adopting your best impatient diva attitude, glide inside.

7. A STAR IS BORN

Tell the promoter you're the assistant to (insert minor celebrity name here), who would like to visit the club that evening. Note: Do not decide to go for broke and name a major star: a) They probably already know Gwyneth's assistant, and you'll only look stupid; and b) you'll have to show up that night with Gwyneth, who's 99.9% certain not to take your calls. We suggest the daughter of a political VIP, which no self-respecting nightlifer would ever recognize. Enlist a friend who has major confidence to play the part of the senator's daughter, and toast each other once inside the club—here's to being sneaky!

SO THERE YOU HAVE IT.

You've learned how to throw a party, deal with an evil landlord and fix even the most heinous of friendship snafus. Your fridge is stocked with gourmet snacks and your wallet's full of money (okay, maybe not full, but at least it's not totally empty). And you can pee standing up better than a lumberjack at a dive bar. (Or maybe you're just reading this page because you're the sort of girl who likes to check out the end of a book before she reads the beginning, in which case, see what you've missed out on? Go back! Read!) Now go out and kick some ass, like the cool girl you know you are.

BELIEVER
IN
HELL

Books by *Wesley C. Baker*
Published by THE WESTMINSTER PRESS

> *Believer in Hell*
> *The Open End of Christian Morals*
> *More than a Man Can Take: A Study of Job*
> *The Split-Level Fellowship*

BELIEVER
IN
HELL

by
WESLEY C. BAKER

THE WESTMINSTER PRESS
Philadelphia

LIBRARY OF CONGRESS CATALOG CARD NO. 68–24676

PUBLISHED BY THE WESTMINSTER PRESS ®

PHILADELPHIA, PENNSYLVANIA

PRINTED IN THE UNITED STATES OF AMERICA

To those loving friends
who waited it out
with patience and trust:

Dave, Roy, Scottie, Marvis,
George, Jim, John

Contents

FIRST REFLECTION   *Paradise Lost*   9
   MOTIF   BROODING   25
   MOTIF   SELF-DECEPTION   33
   MOTIF   DEFEAT   39
   MOTIF   INSULATION   43
   RESOLUTION OF THE MOTIFS   47

SECOND REFLECTION   *The Depressed Priest
Reads His Breviary*   52

THIRD REFLECTION   *Looking at Bedrock*   70
   MOTIF   CREATION   72
   MOTIF   THE FALL   83
   MOTIF   FRATRICIDE   87
   MOTIF   THE DEATH OF CYNICISM   95
   MOTIF   THE IMPOSSIBLE CITY   110
   RESOLUTION OF THE MOTIFS   117

FOURTH REFLECTION   *Death and Resurrection*   119

Paradise Lost

"My life is a house made of paper; any moment my own elbow or that of somebody else will push through it, and the wind will tear the walls to pieces." These words, written anonymously and printed in *Suomen Kuvalehti,* a Helsinki magazine, begin a description of depression from one who knows it only too well.

In England, a pleasant, middle-aged mother perched rather stiffly on the chair in front of her pastor's desk. "I really shouldn't have come here," she began, fiddling with a knotted handkerchief in her lap, "but I seem to have a problem that I can't understand." Then a long, long silence as she tried to hold back the coming storm of tears unsuccessfully.

"I just can't go on," she sobbed. "I have everything any woman could want in life, but I face every day in—*dread.* Oh, whatever shall I do? I'm so alone!"

Into a New England pastor's study that same week came a professionally advanced engineer, father of four, community leader, whose cry for help was just as bewildered and just as pained.

Depression is a living death.

The Finnish writer adds: "Depression is not pretense. It is not an imaginary illness. It is no ordinary sadness or sorrow. Depression is defenselessness, hopelessness, horror of the child who still suffers in the adult. At its deepest it means losing all meaning of life and breaking of all human contacts."

Some of us will respond from the depths of our souls to her poignant comment, "It is despair, almost death."

This writing will not analyze or explain depression. I know neither its cause nor cure. Nor will I be able even to describe it so that others can solve the mystery. It would be most presumptive of me to try to present anything about it clinically, psychologically, medically, that will add anything to the world's understanding. Simply because people who love humanity need to know that some of our brothers' souls are bruised, and in some way need to know *how* they are bruised, I am moved to write.

Dealing with this subject entirely from a background of some religious experience and training, but even more from a foreground of personal affliction, I am only able to *expose* what I can neither understand nor describe. Hopefully, the exposure given more in feeling tone than logic may help someone who cares to care with sympathy, or someone who suffers to feel less alone.

Depression may be the worst of human tragedies, because it is a sickness that estranges its victim from the world, from those he loves, from God, and from himself, yet all the while forcing him to perform the cruel masquerade of living as though he had a soul. Depression is a living death in that it leaves the marks of nonbeing in warm human bodies whose life-resembling motions are endless moments of unendurable, lonely, insistent horror.

Most friends, family, pastors, doctors, deal with this problem with concerned impotence. In most of my ministry, insensitive to the unspeakable agony that imprisoned these souls, I'm afraid I tended to be judgmental, hiding it inside of course. "Oh, come now," I would feel inwardly, "it's all a matter of attitude, you know. You have no real reason to be downcast; it's all in your mind. It's just some way of living that you're not doing right, and you can come out of it any time you really want to. Or perhaps you are treating yourself to the luxury of self-pity, or are calling for attention or affection that you don't think you really deserve."

Outwardly I would be suggesting little morale-building exercises of getting out and mixing with people, of looking at the vast host of those who are worse off than you, or of those who have better reason to be depressed but aren't, or of counting your blessings, and so on.

Then I found myself walking in the valley of the shadow, and it would be a vast understatement to say I was horrified at the remembrance of my earlier prudish capriciousness. Whoever first moaned, "Nobody knows the trouble I've seen," was quite right. Nobody does, especially the healthy.

A depressed person is very sick spiritually. He has become a fundamental atheist, even though he is a professed believer like myself. When the believer goes to hell, he has lost the ability to believe. He cannot tolerate the thought of confrontation with personhood. The idea of God ceases even to be an academic matter for him; just so long as God keeps his distance, he can be if he really wants to be. It just doesn't matter.

It is a terrifying irony that depression is not a fatal disease. A certain mocking, empty kind of existence goes on and on; though everything that makes for real living seems to have been destroyed, the subject involuntarily lives on. And the living process, caught in the momentum of social, family, and professional motion, may even be outwardly productive while inwardly meaningless and absurd.

Sometime ago, a visiting speaker at a college commencement in the West rose above the ordinary, delivering a splendid, incisive, entertaining, and richly inspirational address on "Purposes and Directions." Afterward, appreciative hearers laden with words of praise could not find him; a long search finally ended in the men's washroom. The speaker was in tears and panic; the commendations only made him feel worse. "Please, leave me alone," he moaned. "That speech was for you, not for me. I'm beyond hope. I've given up. Go away!"

It goes the other way, too. Who can imagine the destruction that has been brought into human history because of the living dead? Legend has it that Napoleon was subject to seizures of monumental melancholy, that his appallingly suicidal decisions for empire and battle came out of these glooms. The Bible tells of King Saul of old, whose psychotic spells unleashed hostility against David, and finally destroyed every value he had held dear. Modern historians say much the same about the maxi-tragic figure of Adolf Hitler, and even a daughter's softened reflections, those of Svetlana Alliluyeva, cannot conceal that Stalin spent much time in that valley where there is no rod or staff.

No, no slight slippage of moral principle, this. Nor a matter of moods to be answered with formulas, bromides, or forced cheer. There is something in this malaise that speaks of a disturbance down deep where men find their very being, from which the juices of decision for life or death flow. This is why the whole subject is so mysterious, because it dwells in that unknown Stygian wilderness where existence is either chosen or vetoed. A man in depression is in the anomalous situation of trying to make up his mind whether to live or die, and being without any resources, energy, or care to make a decision in either direction. When the physician talks about a "will to live," or the psychiatrist studies the "death wish," or the social anthropologist ponders the riddle of slum mentality, or the historian tries to rout out the causes of war, they are all asking the same impossible question.

It is my own observation that every human being is a curious contradiction of differing forces toward being and nonbeing. On some lines, we are in healthy contact with reality, eager and capable of responsibilities and interrelations of value. Here the "will to live" is reinforced by feelings of belonging, adequacy, need. But the selfsame person in other areas of his life, or other subjects, may feel inadequate and threatened, or guilty and self-accusatory. A schoolteacher may have remarkable competence in the classroom, yet feel a failure at home. In the one context he is open, alive, honest, and accepting. In the presence of his wife the same man may be evasive, deceptive, and dishonest, that is, death-preferring. The white Southern culture, so warmly hospitable on the one hand and so insensitive to the humanity of the Negro on the other, is a dramatic corporate example of this dichotomy.

Since, then, the degree of our life thrust is only relative, there are variations of the ways we deal with life honestly. Laws of morality and social safety keep us from being completely open and expressive. The masculine sex drive, for instance, given unlimited freedom, would . . . you get the point. Some men acknowledge their libidos and consciously control them; others sublimate deliberately, and others deny. We all have to live in certain kinds of boxes, some of us knowing what we are doing, and others trying very hard not to.

But down beneath it all is the basic mystery. We don't know who man is anyway, and why he would even want to live or die. Both philosophy and theology have an annoying habit of refusing to come up with a final, simple definitive answer, thus the big unknown of what keeps any one of us really wanting to live, really wanting to endure the pain of facing reality and being honest.

And the mystery becomes a paradox only when a man is in trouble with himself, that is, en route to hell.

It wouldn't be so bad in itself, if we could only accept its paradoxical structure and be done with it. But there is an added twinge of absurdity that cannot be ignored. In the need to choose between life and death, it takes just as much affirmation of self to die as to live. Compared with the nonexistence of depression, suicide is affirmative and decisive.

A young man was very prominent in high school activities in a Midwestern town. Faculty and townspeople looked on him with pride, all of them certain that he was going to go far in leadership and human relations. In college, the usual sophomoric slump became a time of complete disillusionment for him from which he never recovered. After deliberately alienating his family and fiancée, and failing in some menial jobs ("He just didn't care enough to try," said one personnel director), he spent twenty years as a "knight of the road," panhandling his necessities along the way. It was his manner always to avoid involvements of meaning and react with snarling hostility when trapped into a prying conversation. "Poor Tom," said those who had known him. "He just didn't know how to live." Wrong. He just didn't know how to die. Or perhaps it could be better put that he thought he'd rather like to try dying but just didn't care enough to pull it off successfully.

There are those who say that alcoholism, narcotics addiction, pathological behavior, and even aggressive social relations are veiled suicide processes, and it makes sense. The key is that the veil is internal, between the person's decision-making center and his own scale of values. He would reject the rational idea of suicide, but his philosophical self has come to the affirmative conclusion that death is a positive choice. The irreconcilability of the two notions has locked into an existential neutrality. The person whose death wish is stronger and more certain will tend to turn to alcohol or other active tools of self-destruction; the person whose deadlock is more even will tend to be depressed. In neither case is the decisive act of suicide a great likelihood; it is that very spurt of courage or assertiveness which the victim of self-divided conflict cannot make.

Strangely, this means that the same dynamics which push a subject toward suicide can also push him toward health. It is the ability to make a decision to do *something*. In his marvelously frank book on life in Harlem, *Manchild in the Promised Land*, Claude Brown tells the story of Danny and his addiction to heroin. Motivated one day by horror over his own attempt to kill his little niece, Danny simply came out of it. He laid aside the habit and never returned to it. The very same motive could have permitted him to destroy himself, but in this case it led to recovery. A nondecision, the more usual course, would have strung it out to the eventual inevitable death which is just an extension of the nonexistence of addiction.

For most, then, it is the inward turning of unresolved conflict that starts the trouble. A psychiatrist friend reasserts Freud's theory that depression is inverted hostility, and this is almost immediately confirmed by one's refusal to accept the image of being a hostile person. So! The repression of an unacceptable self-view is a form of self-deception, and try to live with that while those around you seem to have no problems!

But I don't want to get into psychiatry, since I know it only from the perspective of the couch, not the clipboard, and this writing about depression is from a confessedly nonscientific point of view. I only know that the more adept one becomes at self-deception and the handling of conflict by repression, the more life becomes a tragic shadow. At a recent large meeting of church-women, the program emphasis dealt quite heavily with the world's needs for a redemptive community. The presentation was necessarily stark, with scenes of poverty, defiant and even obscene insults from rebellious youth, discourses on the hostility of disfranchised minorities, criticisms of national and foreign policy. Afterward most of the attending audience maintained they were "depressed," that the meeting hadn't been inspirational as it should have been, and that it had jolly well better be different next year.

Of course they were depressed. It is a normal first reaction to a shattering of preconceived ideas. All healthy human organisms have important shock transitions, and depression belongs here just as grief belongs after the loss of a dear one. It is when any properly transitional adjustment cushion becomes a continuing pattern that it becomes unhealthy.

This women's organization has institutional alternatives that parallel an individual's possibilities. It can stay depressed and demoralized, indecisive about its next meeting, critical of its leadership, and generally incapable of movement anywhere. Or it can throw the whole thing off, disregard the offensive subject matter,

and structure the next meeting along the more traditional, en-
joyable, and less upsetting lines. Its third choice, probably less
likely than either of the first two, is to do an intensive self-
analysis in the light of the world's realities, capitalize on the few
positive reactions, and organize responsibly to effect reconciliation.

In the personal dimension, these same alternatives appear in
much more ambiguous forms. A small-town merchant, who sees
himself as a leading citizen and upholder of morality, is confronted by an employee who points out that the boss has been
consistently unethical and illegal in a certain business practice.
The man can deny it; it isn't his idea of how he really works,
and it must just be a mistake on the clerk's part. Or he can acknowledge it to be true, with a rationalization, or even a shrug
of the shoulders, "So what?" Or, he can be so shocked at the
revelation of a truth he has so successfully hidden from his own
consciousness that he goes into depression. Outwardly, it may
look like either of the first two, but inwardly it can be quite different, with a nondecision for change, a continual denial of the
contradiction, and an alienated life. And, it can be safely predicted, during the time of acute depression, both the moral image
and the illicit practices will continue unresolved.

A member of a symphony orchestra has prided himself for
years on his splendid disciplined and artistic technique. When
the conductor demotes him for incompetency, his first impulse
is to react with hostility, a comparatively normal and healthy
reaction. But since that might evolve into a showdown in which
he might indeed be proven inadequate, he retreats into a silent
sullenness which expresses itself in complete social isolation. He
is a sick man. And in a sense his sickness is the concern of all
men because his reaction is the microcosmic drama of what all
us humans tend to do when fantasy and reality collide. If we
don't care about him in his withdrawal, and see in him a bit of
the retreat of all humanity from its holy callings on earth, we
only invite the despair to engulf us all whenever it will.

Of course, it's too much of an oversimplification to say that depression results from the conflict of reality and fantasy. Sometimes complete fantasies per se get on a collision course, and reality has nothing to do with it. Speaking from an entirely unsophisticated observation of the patterns of youth expressions today such as the hippie movement and the earlier beatnik syndrome, I feel that the "reality" of adult life, the square establishment, has been contrived with an overdose of cynicism. It may, indeed, have all the qualities of hypocritical absurdity that Camus exposed. The prophetic element of this kind of commentary on life has just enough validity to make us all give a Cantinflas-like gesture of acquiescence when the darts are thrown. But a sick commentary does not heal the original sickness, and the hippie (bohemian, gypsy, anarchist, nonconformist, whatever) pattern, in withdrawal from redemptive communication, its hopelessness about the present order of things, and its closing off of appreciation of any values in the dully systematized world, has all the marks of individual depression.

A woman who had been brought up in a fatherless household and taught to regard masculinity with fear and suspicion married a man with homosexual tendencies. Rejoicing in this apparent confirmation of her acquired scorn of men, she encouraged his aberration as a substitute for any kind of meaningful marital associations. When, however, she began to suspect that her husband and her Lesbian partner were having a heterosexual affair, she was in profound emotional conflict. In spite of the (apparently truthful) denials of the accused pair, the neurotic wife had no way to ease out of her box without surrendering a primary fantasy. Her moods of depression became so intense that there was no ordinary way to make contact, and she had to be institutionalized. In like manner do the fantasies of sex, acquisitiveness, security, and social recognition drive many of us into corners where *every* wall is an unreality, either forced upon us by emotional conditioning or corporate fairly tale.

Another woman writes: "Once I spent a day at home by myself. This is by no means unusual although I am no hermit except in deep depression. That time I was not even restless but full of happy, practical plans. A woman can so enjoy some spare time when she has, for instance, some nice material to be sewn, or beautiful blue paint to be used. In the middle of this bustle something struck my mind. What am I really doing right now? Am I not just killing time while I wait for this life to end—this often almost unbearable life? In a minute I was in the darkest landscape of my soul."

This is the deep enigma of depression. Busy, happy, intelligent minds can, in turning over the proper subjects for review, suddenly become poisoned and crippled. Yet for her, at this certain time, the question of the meaning of life and existence was not a proper one, for she was not emotionally prepared to deal with it. The whole mental procedure was a collision of fantasies, the underlying fantasy being that since she was happy with her homebody chores, she was ready to find answers to the fundamental questions of life. Looking at the incident through her own description, one can make a good horseback guess and say that in the first place she wasn't really *happy*, she was just pleasantly distracted. And in the second, she didn't honestly come to grips with existence; the subject proved to be but a screen on which she projected her own profoundly disturbed inadequacy to be human. And suddenly she was in hell.

I have nothing at all to suggest what she might have done in that case, for I don't understand the dynamics; I only can identify at the pain level and know not only *how* it happened in the viscera, but that it *did* happen. I can only suggest that it would have been better not to be alone, and it's a very weak thing to say at that. It is a terrible thing for a person who is a victim of this disease to be alone and unprepared. The writer of the Old Testament book of Ecclesiastes, cynic and pessimist that he was, must certainly have known more about basic humanity than most of us. He writes: "Two are better than one, because they have a good reward for their toil. For if they fall, one will lift up his fellow; *but woe to him who is alone when he falls and has not another to lift him up."* (Eccl. 4:9, 10; italics added.)

Not that people don't get depressed when surrounded by loving admirers; the modern phrase "lonely in a crowd" is an accurate possibility. It is rather to say that when the descent into hell begins, one casts a furtive, helpless, fearful glance back to see if there is one outstretched hand that might at the last moment stop the slide. If a friend had been sitting in her sewing room, chatting gaily, she just *might* have dropped the word of assurance, or even reproof, that would at least have broken the pathological train of thought. Depression is a desperately, miserably, soul-chillingly lonely condition, for it is characterized by the building of protective walls that prove always to be a cruel prison.

The servants of King Saul of long ago knew this. They observed that "the Spirit of the Lord departed from Saul, and an evil spirit from the Lord tormented him" (I Sam. 16:14). So they persuaded him to send for a musician to be with him in his dark moods, to play healing music. So came David, the sweet-singing shepherd boy, and "Saul loved him greatly, . . . and whenever the evil spirit from God was upon Saul, David took the lyre and played it with his hand; so Saul was refreshed, and was well, and the evil spirit departed from him." (vs. 21, 23.) Don't draw too many conclusions from the fact that the story of Saul ends tragically. To those of us who have tasted the "evil spirit from God," the simple appearance of this so very authentically human story is in itself a value beyond description. It is fuel to the furnaces of survival to know that the mighty tradition of Israel got under way by having a depressive as its first king. Never mind what happened to him; we don't really care what happens to us. Just the assurance that there is some value somewhere—somehow even in the lives that dwell in hell—is a mighty significant bellwether.

Now we have come full circle around to the basic meditations upon the mysterious puzzle "to be or not to be." It doesn't take

Danish royalty alone to see that it is a question no man can
answer by himself. It's not that the sick people get sicker when
they try to discover the meaning of life, and the healthy are immune. No man, whatever his emotional condition, can probe
that abyss without getting badly frightened, or badly hurt, or
tumble into hell, or die. I just don't believe that some can travel
that path and escape unscathed; instead, the healthy know when
to turn back, or the questions not to ask. They don't go so far
into it with their vulnerable life nerves exposed. They blend into
vapid generalities that leave the specific self untouched, and they
come back with their eyes shining as if they had really been there,
but they *haven't.* Those of us, like Saul (the record shows him to
be the only Biblical character who sought out a witch to make
personal contact) and like our lady friend above, who asked the
unforgivable questions unprotected, found no reward for our
search but the slipping of gravel under our feet in the dark. No
wonder "absurdity" is the cry of a generation whose favorite in-
door sport is to pick each other's brain about the sense of existence!

Yet we all somehow have to wonder about life, and build a
treasury of confidence in the essential direction of life. Some of
the questions have to be asked, but lightly, brother, lightly. And
the answers make their real appearance in the insistent process
of living itself, not in forms that can be outlined, volumed, and
lectured, but in hunches, feelings, unprovoked awarenesses. They
come as gifts, and one should never look a gift horse in the you
know what. All of which leads one to comment that a person who
can fall victim to depression is a very special kind of human
being. He is supersensitive and overresponsive to the injurious
soul-scratches of life. Even though his symptom of disease is
withdrawal and apparent imperviousness, he got that way by
being too exposed, too involved, too interested in life. He
bounced out of the womb with his heart on his sleeve, eager to
find out, to enjoy, to be fulfilled. Rather than being oblivious to
the things that put life together, he wanted to know too much;
he asked too damned many questions. And when his trust was

answered, either in fancy or for real, with rebuff and rejection, he became a heroic casualty. Jan Masaryk and James Forrestal came back to health long enough to commit creative suicide, Søren Kierkegaard to make systematic sense of despair (and psychic suicide?), and Karl Marx, like Faustus of yore, sold his soul to the devil. But most of us are wounded just so deeply that we peer at our imaginative brothers through a thick veil that keeps their prying curiosities at a safe distance, and wish we had the courage to die.

The real question is, of course, the psalmist's words, "What is man?" It really is a very hard pill to swallow that "Thou hast made him little less than God," when I don't even have the contentment of the dog asleep in my lap. Does being man mean that I must always exist with this existential vacuum, this guilt for a destiny unfulfilled, this call to bear unjust burdens? Why couldn't I have been a dog?

During the Alabama racial crises of 1963, I walked the streets of Montgomery and Selma arm in arm with black men, seeking to alleviate my own outrage at the blasphemous disregard for human justice that I knew dwelt as much in me as in any man. One of my assigned duties in that unstructured army of volunteers was to call on some of the local clergymen. We were trying to put white flesh where black flesh hurt, to taste of the pathos and in sharing the injustice, make way for a new justice.

In the study of one large downtown church in Montgomery I tried to relate to my professional brother on nonthreatening and mutually accepting terms. He was gracious, courteous, and very distant.

"I've come," I began, "as a fellow minister of the gospel to stand with you in our mutual concerns for justice and obedience to Christ."

"That's very good of you."

"What do these events mean for the churches of Montgomery? How can the rest of us be of help to you in your ministry of reconciliation?"

"Well, now," he smiled and leaned back in his swivel chair.

"Now that you ask, I suggest you go home. The first thing we need is the restoration of law and order. Then the churches and the good citizens of Alabama will work together for the good of all people."

"What have you been doing for the last hundred years?"

"I'm sure we've been doing just what Jesus would want us to do. We love our brothers, we help them in their need, and we denounce such extremists as the Ku-Klux Klan."

"Specifically," I pressed, "what will you do tomorrow, if the civil rights workers leave town, that you haven't done before?"

"Why, we will continue to give our Negro brothers all kinds of opportunities to have a good life."

"Why haven't you good church people of the South done that already?"

"I think you'll find," he said softly, "that we have. Over and over again. The Negro here in Montgomery is better off than he is in Chicago or Harlem, by far. This whole fuss is caused by outsiders, even well-meaning preachers like yourself, used by professional revolutionaries and conspirators. Our colored folk were doing quite well until you came along."

"How close are you to Negroes? Do you associate with them on an equal basis?"

"We southerners are closer to Negroes, and understand them better than anyone else."

"Are there Negro members in your church?"

"They prefer to go to their own, only two blocks from here."

"Have you ever been inside a Negro home?"

"I make pastoral calls wherever I'm invited."

"Do you feel that Negroes are treated unjustly?"

"I've always been good to them."

"What specific reforms will you and your church work for in helping dignity and justice to come to your Negro neighbors?"

"This church will be faithful always to the Bible and the gospel. I preach Christ and him crucified; that is my calling. Good day, sir. Thank you for coming."

There was just no way I could guide the conversation into honest channels; he firmly redirected every question to safe ground. I found myself on the street feeling that my mission was a total failure. The stupid irony of that whole scene is that it was I who went away depressed, and he probably got a good night's sleep!

But in all charity, it has to be said that if he for a moment let his guard down, in the face of his own rather impressive Biblical scholarship, he might have come unglued, and that right messily. Given all the considerations of that context, he did the only thing he could without the horrendous consequences of death, depression, or monumental change. I would almost admire his strength if it weren't for the fact that he maintained his survival at the expense of his humanity. For to repress the obvious moral pressures of the rather unambiguous situation, he had to be less than a man; that's the only way anyone can escape identifying with another man's suffering. In a sense, he was making the decision not to be human in that certain area, for the cost was too great.

Lest this sound too judgmental on one man or one culture, I hasten to say that we all do this in some measure and in perhaps some different dimensions. When we hear a news flash that so many innocent civilians have been made homeless, or killed, in a village in Vietnam, or as the result of another Israel-Arab foray, or in a riot in the streets of Hong Kong, and toss it off lightly, we are doing the same thing—we are forsaking our humanity. To carry that even farther, life is a series of humanity-denying survival measures, such as turning into a personless lump of wood on an elevator, avoiding direct eyeball contact, pretending to be otherwise occupied. Or it is the maneuver of shielding one's self behind a role or uniform in the performance of an appointed task so that no valuable time or costly emotional juice is unwisely invested. It's all part of the same tactic that my Alabama counterpart used, and it's really very necessary to keep us from drowning in nonessential overinvolvement. The point

being made here is that it is only done at a price to the integral
unity of personality; one must always be aware of how much he
is paying for his privacy and be willing to understand the peril
of overspending. I call this game "selective humanity."

The point of bankruptcy in selecting our humanity too closely
is depression. Each little play in the game consists of throwing
up a veil, a temporary bit of film that distorts the outsider's view
of the inside. But portable as it is intended to be, each piece of
veil has in it elements of a wall; translucence leads to opaque-
ness, and ere the protected really understands what is happening,
he is a prisoner entrapped in his own defense system. He can't
see out.

In telling the tale of the interview in Dixie, then, I was por-
traying myself on another plane, impervious to the lines I was
drawing for myself. My own awareness of being was cramped
way down somewhere. It served me right for capitalizing on a
situation that had all the earmarks of clear-cut righteousness.

But can we afford to be sensitive to the things that hurt others?
This is one of the contradictory backlashes of human interaction.
We only really love, honestly enter into relationships of meaning
with other persons in proportion to the way we can identify,
share, understand. Health and wholesomeness characterize the
letting down of the guard, the ability to vibrate with others'
shakennesses, the quality of sensitiveness. This is, in a way, the
lending out of your own treasury of stability at high risk on the
gamble that the contact "out there" will enrich the capital gain
in someone else. But unforeseen elements can crop up from any
direction, and it is the one who has invested the most who can
be hurt the worst. What I am saying is that it is sensitive, caring
types that are most liable to be depression victims. The paradox
here is that the depressed one *appears* to be withdrawn, to care
no more, to be only half alive, to be alone in hell. He really is,
but he got that way precisely because he wasn't that kind of guy.
It is the brotherhood of the pain in the gut who somehow know
why Jesus was so surly before Pilate, and why he cried out, "My

God . . . why?" Disappointing as that performance may be to the idealists and the purists, it comes through to some of us as an authentication of the whole story in terms we know so very well. We know *too* well.

For most of us, depression isn't just a once-in-a-lifetime event, a time of trouble and a success story to relate as a thing of the past. It's pushing on into life with a recurring possibility around the next corner, an insistent succession of irregular cycles enacting a profound drama about life and existence and us that we just don't understand. It's quite clear to us that nobody else understands it, either. It all seems so unexplainable, so irrational, so unjust, that others can smile and laugh, and face tomorrow with confidence.

That's why it's hell, in the full theological description of a very well informed and thoroughly human Scriptural expression. Hell, in New Testament terms, is the condition of being separated from God. Alienated, walled off, estranged. Hell.

MOTIF

BROODING

The tendency to scratch the new scab off an old wound so that it continues to bleed and hurt may be a form of masochism, whatever that is. But it's still a puzzling phenomenon. "Worrying" is the process of repetitive reviewing of disastrous alternatives with no clear awareness that they may be mostly imaginary. The most morbid symptom of depression is the compulsion to dwell on the gloomiest possibility that the mind could conjure at such length and intensity that it becomes the only development that could happen.

One would think that the practice of brooding is so irrational that anyone with any kind of logic could talk himself out of it easily. Not so; it is the rational mind that seems to be seduced the quickest, and there are no bootstraps available. There's an old classical joke about the man who was sent by his wife to go next door and borrow a saucepan. En route, the obedient husband mulls over in his mind the possible negative attitude with which he *might* be met at the neighbor's door thusly: "He'll probably be watching TV, and the doorbell will annoy him. He doesn't know me and very likely won't want me for a friend. Stupid guy! Won't even give me a chance." So, when the door opens, he can only shout, "I didn't want your damned old saucepan anyway!"

I once knew a man who studied law, with no little ability. But after five tries he still hadn't passed the state bar examinations; his brooding became a self-fulfilling prophecy. He would study until he became emotionally exhausted and depressed, then brood about inevitable failure. He brought it upon himself, for in his better moments his grasp of the subject matter appeared more than adequate to accredited lawyers.

Imagined infidelity on the part of a mate or lover, rehearsed fears of loss of money or security, wild wonderings about social acceptability, and a whole host of grotesque mythological unrealities parade back and forth, back and forth, back and forth, through the mind of the sickest of us. Sometimes all night long, sometimes while we are at work, or carrying on the motions of that world out there, they go like subtitles on a movie screen, or lurk like shadows behind every door, or sit beside us on the front seat of the car and chatter in our ear like a talkative wife.

Because of the macabre element of dialogue, even argument, that a brooder has to keep up with these dismal fantasies, we understand the dynamics of demonology. To say that a man is possessed of an evil spirit is just about the only way to explain it, or rather describe it. It's like there's another self, a demonic fragment of our own whose job is to jab mercilessly with that sharp fork.

This mysterious "otherness" about the brooding spirit is an uncanny experience. I have been in meetings with a group of nice people, when suddenly I am aware that there is another presence in the room; it is a very frightening and terribly dismaying thought. I become chilled all over, from head to toe, and I groan silently, "No, not that again!" The brooding begins and contact with the group gets to be more and more of an effort. Someone speaks, asks a question, and it takes a mighty struggle of thought muscle to hear and respond, even with a quip. But the demon isn't waylaid. He just moves around to the other ear, or down into my aching chest, and goes about his cruel work. He may stay for ten minutes, or rack my aching spirit for two or three days. He never really goes away; there are just those merciful intervals when he catches a little sleep. When the poor fellow in Gerasa was confronted by Jesus, no wonder he cried out, "I beseech you, do not torment me" (Luke 8:28). He'd had enough of the horror. Again, we who have walked the paths of the Gerasene countryside see no inconsistency whatever in the dispatching of the demons into the herd of swine. They're that real to us.

There ought to be many things that could be said to the brooder. On the face of it, it looks so ridiculous and uncivilized that just a little of some kind of self-discipline should do the whole thing in. But after you've said, "Come now, it's all in your mind. Think positively!" there isn't much left. Again, we take some kind of comfort in the Biblical insight in which demons are never chased out by sheer determination; it is the external influence of Christ's healing power, or the presence of the concerned community or the corporate therapy of a church intent on releasing into the world the power of a Holy Spirit, which, like the wind, can be neither seen nor controlled, only experienced as a gift. We brooders try until we are utterly exhausted to dispatch the demon, and frequently the very weariness from our efforts lets the infection deepen and we become sicker. When help comes, it is a gift. None of us know any more than to endure until relief comes.

I have even tried a little humor in the manner of lighting a candle to dispatch the darkness. "Oops!" I've cried out, sometimes aloud to the surprise of my companions. "There you go

again. Quick, Henry, the Flit!" Or, when the good missus asks
if there's anything she can get for me, my stock answer is, "Yes,
a gun with one bullet in it."

But it doesn't seem to help, except to give a momentary distraction, which only seems to delay the getting on with it. Was it
Mark Twain who said that a cold would last a fortnight if left
alone, and if treated by a doctor would last only two weeks? You
get the picture.

Surely, there ought to be some value to sublimation, that is,
busying oneself with happy activity or immersing oneself in social
contacts and healing friendships. Haven't basket-weaving and
violin-playing brought myriads of people back from the brink?
I don't know. I think I've tried nearly everything, including book-
writing. It does help, of course, in a functional way, and ought
never be discounted as a viable possibility, but on the other hand
it should never be prescribed as a sure cure. There have been so
many parties, and nights on the town, and social evenings with
friends, or gala formal public occasions that I went through with
pleasantness all over the outside and pain on the inside that the
memory alone is wearying. How often, in the sheer desperate
struggle of trying to keep the whole schmier from being a depressing disaster to the other loving people around me, have I
just turned my soul off and my artificial front on just to *endure
the time.* This pertains even when the party was planned for me
by those who cared. Always, it would be something to appreciate
and cherish, and stow away as another of those needed assurances
on which life feeds. All the while, it felt as though it took more
effort than it was worth.

"Occupational therapy" is what the professionals call any kind
of activity that will draw a person out of a gloomy corner. I believe in it wholeheartedly; I have spent enough time visiting
mental hospitals and emotionally-ill friends to know that it has
many values. It has a particular feature, like physical therapy, of
demanding the dedicated attention of at least one other person
who with his time and presence reaches his hand over the fence

to you and holds it warmly while you struggle to respond. Often the response is not due to the techniques the therapist is using, but just to the fact that he's there and seems to be an incarnation of all personal mankind; his outstretched hand means everything.

This is why I cannot discount sublimating attempts, whether they come from inside as an indication of a will to claim the human heritage, or from concerned friends. I just want to insist that they are not necessarily always successful. What if I had taken every attack by the brooder demon by sitting in the darkened basement with my head in my hands? It may be surprising to report that I feel there would be just as much health or sickness now as there is in me anyway.

A major reason for this is that the demons are invisible to loving friends. Whatever the outsiders try to do, they don't know the enemy they're trying to destroy, and they can become all too easily frustrated. "What you need," they'll say, with large compassion, "is a stiff drink." Or a whole day fishing, or a good night's sleep. Maybe all I need is to be left alone, or a night on Bald Mountain, or—what the hell.

There was that long meeting, some years ago; it went all day and into the night. There were twenty or thirty professional cohorts there, all personal friends. There was much patter, interaction, group thinking, jokes in machine-gun order, and big items cared for in responsible manner. I was secretary, but inside my solar plexis the battle of Iwo Jima was undergoing a rerun in technicolor and stereophonic sound. Every demon in my personal posse was there; oh, God, it hurts too much even now to try to describe it. But there was no way out of the box. Had I fled to protected privacy, the terror inside would not have let up. So I stayed and the meeting was a grand success. At the adjournment, there was hardly enough of me left to make it to the car, and when I got there with the cheerful voices left behind, I was left alone with those goddamned goading demons, each one screaming shrilly, "What if . . . !" I beat the steering wheel and bawled. The next day a very good friend, who is possibly the most aware of my problem, remarked in an offhand way, "You were a little quiet yesterday, but it was good having the old you back with us."

No, don't let me derail you by my use of the word "demon." There is no attempt here to pass the whole syndrome off as an attack from outer space on grand innocence. Demons are not "other," even though I represent that the effect of brooding is one of being aggravated from outside. Those demons are all me, the pointed barbs of some mysteriously self-destructive traits in my psyche, and I know it. It may not be the same kind of inner war that Paul describes in the seventh chapter of the epistle to the Romans, but it's the same bewildering sensation. The plain truth is that the Achilles' heel of my soul (or my sense of being a person, or whatever you want to call it) is a compulsive over-concern that my own messianic or superman image not be shattered. So I play games with other people to keep the images captive. Since I am not God (a proposition sometimes hard to accept), the big things are out of my control, and I worry about losing the whole shooting match. If this sounds sick to you, believe me, it's even worse to me. Knowing all this doesn't necessarily bring the magic Freudian release promised in holy psychiatry. Those damned demons still come. As each one screams, I can answer him with dynamic explanations and powerful put-downs galore. *But he doesn't go away!*

The medieval folklore about evil spirits is curiously helpful here. The legend goes that these malevolent personages are immune to any kind of ordinary human interference in their impious mischief. They seemed to be able to break through to king or peasant; their plagues could bring insanity to the villages, haunting to the castles, and panic to the masses. A complicated system of amulets, charms, and magic potions confessedly fell short of guaranteeing a demon-free existence. There was one thing, however, universally acknowledged to ward off the evil spirit from the final kill: a crucifix or plain cross. Just to hold this symbol up to be seen is to send the unwanted visitor crashing through the forest in his own form of terror, "No, not that!"

Somewhere, down deep, I feel that there is more flesh-and-blood authentic human experience behind this fireside narration than meets the eye. No, no, I'm not cluttering my mysticism with Gothic cobwebs, not going to put a silver crucifix around my neck in the shower. But I do feel that when the peasants put this little bit of jollity together, they were trying to say something they had a collective idea about, concerning the terrors of a frightened lonely human spirit, trying to make sense out of the forward motion of life, and what the visitation of emotional infections may reflect about God and man. I believe that the witchcraft cults, black masses, and general folklore about the occult are rooted as much in the struggle for health as they are in the morbid, and that the demons they feared were by and large the same fraternity that visited me in that committee room.

Which brings us, then, to the symbolism of the crucifix and its magic powers of dispatch. Beneath the considerable layer of non-Christian folk tradition and superstition, the imagery of the forest primeval, there is a supratheological cumulative response to medieval teaching of Christ and the atonement that appears here in a rather remarkable way. Somehow, this reveals, medieval man felt that the answer to the loss of any person's humanity is to be found in the revelation of what humanity really is. When all the hocus-pocus of the appeals to the nonhuman world have run their course and are found to be only half-answers, then the appeal is not to the world farthest out but to the place where man is really, fully man.

Whatever gibes we modern men may take at the nonrational and even unreasonably cruel types of religious faiths of a millennium ago, we cannot overlook that at the points of genuine testing, when all the cards were on the table and man really had to be with it, medieval man came through. The semimythical representations of Christ were nearly too human for our protected sophistications; lifelike images dangled over European altars with gory wounds in the side and dripping blood. Or, representations of the "sacred heart" made modern color-TV broadcasts of heart surgery look like Band-Aid commercials. No generation of Christian history has so deeply explored the facets of the hurting human soul as can be seen in any of the thousands of *Pietàs* painted, carved, molded, chiseled, in the Middle Ages. In a way that no historian can possibly clarify, nor cultural anthropologist ever label, there was an identification of man with himself in those times, in which the symbols of captive Christianity, which seem so unreal to us, came through in blazing light and warmth.

Some of them, undoubtedly including emperors, bishops, burghers, and peasants, knew what it was to be in hell. And to them the crucifix, or any symbol that suggested that God also knew what it was to be himself hurt, did more to injure the demonic cause than anything else. So when I read, even in the current Dracula-type vampire stories, about the mystic powers of the crucifix, always resulting in a restored humanity, I nod my head. I fully believe that any symbol which evaporates the shadows and puts man eyeball-to-eyeball with Complete Man, made nonthreatening because that Complete Man also hurts as I hurt, dispatches demons.

Why, then, can we not use this type of therapy now? Perhaps we can, but there are many complications. The modern mind has a whole different system of myth symbols. They explore the human spirit in very different dimensions, and there really is no complete symbol in the twentieth century that represents the purity of man and the suffering of God as the Middle Ages saw the cross. Where they yearned for eternal security, we search for temporal comfort. If we were confronted with a representation of humanity at its best, the chances are that it would collide so fiercely with our fantasies that we would be more threatened and repelled than healed. So the crucifix bit is out, but the possibility of being helped by knowing what we might be is still therapeutic.

Whether or not modern man goes to church, he is tired of the hortatory mood in everything addressed to him. The phrases "we ought, we must, you need, if only, somehow we've got to," laminating together a bewilderment at cold war, Vietnam, napalm standoffs, make us want to clap our hands over our ears. In this context, any representation of authority is just another loud accusatory voice, strong in bleatings about our failure, but not equipped with a sacrament of penance that can wash us clean first.

This is my problem. I give strong personal assent to Christian theology that upholds the incarnation as the crossroads of the human and the divine, and I know from the best of my rational resources that here is a characterization of my sickness and my healing. But emotionally I am an atheist, sturdily unwilling to let my protected privacy be invaded by any caricature of what I'm supposed to be, when I don't really even care very much about what I am now, and whether or not it's a genuine fragment of what I might be. Brooding, then, becomes a way of *simulating* life, because of the pain. To corrupt the Cartesian well, "I hurt, therefore I am." This gruesome and pathetic way of existing without existence, of purging guilt without forgiveness, creates its own need for continuation, becomes addictive.

Incredible, isn't it? It's about the only way I can put it down on paper, and even then most of it is untold. We brood, the demons scream their ludicrous obscenities, and the fires of hell encompass us. Yet somewhere, somehow, there is a fullness of man that can come to us and, like the monstrance of the Holy Cross of old, exorcise.

MOTIF

SELF-DECEPTION

Kierkegaard certainly knew what the inside of hell looked like, though the angst in which he writes may be more related to health than sickness. One of his most sublime writings bore the title "Purity of Heart Is to Will One Thing." The "one thing" he admonishes us to pursue is the will of God, not just as a pious exercise, but as the only way to make any sense at all out of life.

One feels that he is well aware of the internal damage caused by willing more than one thing, or even worse, contradictory things. This is called self-deception, a sure road to paralysis of the soul.

Again, this is something that makes no sense whatever. Why we constantly fall into the temptation of living in different worlds at once makes good subject matter for satirical cartoonists, but no helpful conclusions for historians. It may be some comfort, but not much, to us who hurt ourselves privately in this way to know that it seems also to be a corporate characteristic.

The chief evidence here is war, the use of international hostilities to gain short-range goals. If a person were to apply the logic of historical determinism to man, seeing him through the monumental developments such as industrial and technological revolutions, he would feel safe in predicting that good leadership would prevail upon the human race to rise above the primitiveness and obsolete methodologies of war. Indeed, at a World Peace Congress in Chicago in 1911, a new "civilized" peaceful era of human existence was happily proclaimed.

It never came off. We are too collectively self-deceptive. One remembers George Bernard Shaw's comment that if there is indeed life elsewhere in the universe, God must surely be using earth as a cosmic insane asylum. Even the most healthy among us behave like those in the Rotary Club in your town, meeting under the motto "Service Above Self." Yet out of a sampling of any hundred Rotarians, business and professional men of the community, the cutting edge of "American" culture, selfless motives wouldn't even appear in the top ninety. Men are Rotarians (including yours truly) because of profitable contacts, the gratifying of certain social needs, and to have another resource with which to fulfill certain limited personal goals. Curiously, Rotary started off in the first decade of the twentieth century at least honestly stating its aims in a you-scratch-my-back-and-I'll-scratch-yours declaration. But that kind of honesty too easily stirs up feelings of guilt, so it had to be changed.

Rotary is a microcosmic parable of the prevailing winds today.

As a cultural twist, it can be taken in stride, but for some of us, the carrying of the syndrome into the personal-living realm provokes a deteriorating grip on integrity, and a journey into hell.

Self-deception is the "wishing will make it so" mentality. A wife and mother saw herself as the completely devoted, ever-loving model of what womanhood is all about. The fact that she drove her husband and children to distraction by making a show of her selflessness had long ago ceased to be funny. As a matter of fact, it was only too apparent to family and friends that she was basically a very self-centered person, cannily manipulating those around her into double binds to serve her ends. This kind of maneuver wasn't all that subconscious; in fact, it was rather keenly planned by a woman who knew quite well what she was doing. But inside, there was no attempt to reconcile the irreconcilable. She was happy with her image and happy with her methods, and lost no sleep over trying to make them match.

The danger of this is that when the day of judgment, in the form of some kind of self-exposure comes, there is no defense, absolutely none. The only tactic for survival, beyond denial which is a continuing deception, is withdrawal. When Captain Ahab finally caught up with his Moby Dick, there was nothing left to live for, so he just had to go to the bottom with his whale, lashed a hundred strands over by the tangled harpoon line.

It is often said that the preacher who condemns adultery the loudest is the one who's most likely to get caught at it someday. Psychologists say that any strong and hostile gesture of disapproval, such as the Carry Nation crusade against John Barley-corn, betrays a repressed longing for the freedom to relate to that very sin guilt-free. When father, down East, ordered his pregnant unmarried daughter out into the snow, it was the only possible action open to him in which he could show his strong feelings of dismay and, surprisingly, compassion. It is a strong probability that many people marry, not for love, but in a self-deceiving act of masochistic guilt atonement, or a display of sheer antisexual hostility. All of which wouldn't be so bad if we weren't a society that insisted on a purity of motive that implies dishonor to all else.

The Vietnam enigma also has to be seen in this light. The U.S.A., still affected by the "manifest destiny" psychology, has impressed upon itself such a strong messianic image and has centered its corporate feelings of well-being around the proposition that history, righteousness, and Almighty God cannot possibly get along without the red, white, and blue, that we just can't believe there isn't some purifying touch to our guns in the jungle. We have to account for our many stupendous blessings by accepting our holy calling to be the savior of the world. It matters not that the issues are confused; our very participation ought to clear all that up, for we are always on the right side against the forces of evil.

We are the victims of our own monstrous self-deception. We have never stopped to examine our own real motives, to see how our own nationalistic narcissism looks from outside, or even to clarify whether we are really interested so much in saving the world as we are in preserving the fantasy. What is the fate of a nation, whatever its strengths and riches, that pursues its imaginary path like an army of two hundred million Don Quixotes?

One of San Francisco's most beloved legends is that of Emperor Norton. This friendly simpleton walked the streets by the Golden Gate nearly a century ago, wearing an imperialistically gaudy uniform, insisting that he was supreme sovereign of the city. The warmth in this story is that the city played the game with him, publishing his edicts (mostly proclamations of holidays), giving him entry into social and public occasions, even free meals in the restaurants. He lived a long and happy life, never once having to deal with his slight misjudgment of the realities, and San Francisco pleased itself with the protection of its loyal friend from ever being told otherwise. It is a delightful slice of the human story in all its aspects, but more because of an understanding and tolerant society than that a certain man prevailed in his grandiose dreams. Even if we lived in a world that accepted us lovingly whatever we were, if we lived a lie, we would still be sick.

Emperor Norton's great advantage was that he was too far gone to know the difference. Most of us who indulge in the luxury of self-deception live closer to painful insight, so ours is a precarious existence.

The story of Brother Norton does introduce the wonderful element of humor, and how it may be an instrument of adjustment as no other. The writers of the Biblical books of Ruth and Jonah, and of the story of Samson, were by no means the first humorists whose whole ministry comprised the lifting up of a mirror and letting the rest of us see the unexpected ridiculous.

What Mark Twain, Gilbert and Sullivan, Art Hoppe, and Dick Gregory are to their societies, some small inside voice could be to us. There was a time when a certain public figure was exerting considerable damage on his constituency by misinterpreting his role in history. His loyal cohorts wondered how to call his attention to the problem without angering or hurting him. Their job was done for them by a newspaper cartoonist who depicted the situation incisively with the central figure, our Mr. X, appearing so inept as to be a thorough buffoon. When he saw it, he said, "By George, he's right!" and roared with laughter. Later, the cartoonist received an award for effecting the arrival of badly needed insight.

I well remember, in the midst of a time of leading a psychically double life, catching a glimpse of myself by accidentally overhearing a conversation not meant for my ears. "If he only knew," said somebody who knew what he was talking about, "how funny he looks to us." It *was* funny, and fortunately at that minute I could laugh, but there have been a hundred other occasions when humor was one of those things I was avoiding. Subconsciously, I would rather have been an Emperor Norton. It is gratifying to see that some famous people, like President Franklin D. Roosevelt, were able to accept the critical gibes in laughable packages. At F.D.R.'s order, the museum in his honor at Hyde Park preserves several well-remembered examples.

A married man who has a mistress with whom he is genuinely
involved emotionally has put himself into a world of self-deception. Neither socially acceptable alternative appeals to him:
divorce and remarriage to live with the bloody stump of guilt
and inner accusation, or voluntarily severing the meaningful but
clandestine relationship. So he tries to string it along as far as
possible, leading a double life, promising each woman either
that all is well, or things will soon go her way. In actuality, down
deep he is keeping a good thing going as is, and is unwilling to
pay the price of change. All the while he is telling himself that
it is a proper situation and he is capable of dealing with it in
good order. Some men, in this fix, do resort to one of the necessary choices as a way of escaping depression.

Somewhere in that time of terrible transition known as adolescence there is a cataclysmic rehearsal of self-deception. It centers
around either academic performance or social relationships. It is
a time of high and noble idealism, which must of necessity be
uncluttered by too much realism. It is a time to dream, but it
also is the time to start being exasperated in impatience. It may
be that, like homosexuality, there is a phase of growing in which
self-deception is a normal and even desirable behavior pattern,
so that it can be evaluated in the whole learning process. College
campuses have always been the sites of revolution, of innovation,
defiance, and excess. Very few adults remember their teen-age
years clearly, or understand the acutely agonizing developments
of those times. Evidently it is the adult role to be quite out of
the sphere of transitional youth, so that we can reflect with
reality how we react. Youth can then measure its fantasies against
the world that is, and hopefully see the traces where they have
been kidding themselves. After all, if all society were to treat
the hippies the way San Francisco treated Emperor Norton, it
would just be another way of building a glass hothouse around
the disease and preserving it.

But what about those of us who are adult in years, and are
still bothered by this adolescent symptom? Can it be that we are

the victims of arrested development, and that it is our need to grow up? If so, how does one do his own growing up? Probably by staying in honest contact with the world, and in open and frank relationship with other people, and by an overhauling of all fantasies. What a depressing thought!

M O T I F

DEFEAT

Because defeat means the failure of something positive, it has to be in a major key. Defeat only comes to those who try, and who try to win at that. But also because defeat is so overwhelming, so crushing, it has to be depicted in terms of broad, overwhelming and stately waves.

In depression one tastes defeat. Or rather, it might be better said that one interprets life in terms of defeat. A healthier person might interpret the very same circumstances differently, considering them a setback, or a challenge, or even victory. But the depressed person has taken such a beating that he has thrown in the towel and doesn't even care enough to stick around to see his opponent's glove lifted high.

Defeat, then, is more a state of mind than an external fact. Nonetheless, it is very real, oppressively true, and a bringing to a numbed and incredulous halt of any further attempts to prevail. Its subtitles are: "I've had it." "I've lost it all." "I quit!"

Here defeat doesn't apply so much to projects, or campaigns to bring visible results, as it does to the sheer effort one makes to be a person, to make sense out of life, to attain a certain measure of emotional balance and well-being. It's because these fights are the basic elements of sanity and existence that defeat means a declaration of *nolo contendere* to just staying alive in any worthwhile sense. This means that it is several points the other side of suicide, which is not so much defeat as it is a defiant last spurt of aggressive resistance. It *is* suicide in the category of fleeing from keeping up the fight on the terms of this world, but it is *not* suicide in that it doesn't even possess the courage or determination to take such innovative action.

When a large supermarket chain opened three new stores in a Southern city, the neighborhood grocers, faced with the kind of competition that could only drive them into bankruptcy, reacted in several different ways. Some organized a small grocers' cooperative which meant, at great sacrifice to them, staying in business by putting prices down and hanging by the skin of their financial teeth. This is healthy defiance. Others closed their shops in protest, appealing to the public not to permit such injustices to the free-enterprise American way of life. This is hostile suicide. A third group, indecisive, simply stayed in business on the old terms, as though the competition weren't there, going under with the ultimate and inevitable when it came. They just didn't care enough to take a positive step up or down. This is defeat.

A successful salesman told his wife that he wanted a divorce, giving her custody of the two teen-age sons. Since he had practically no grounds, she could have resisted, held her ground, and kept the home together. Or, she could have consented to the divorce, and on the basis of his generous income, would have been clearly able to maintain the home and raise the boys in financial security, giving her opportunity to create a new life of her own. Instead, she was so taken aback by the implied failure of her womanness that she chose to ignore both the request and any further hurtful relation to him. Her inaction and indecision cost her everything, for when the judge saw her total apathy, he took the children from her and reduced her alimony. To this day she lives in a withdrawn and sterile world, rejecting all implications and memories. Though she feels hostile, she is unable to bring it to any kind of expression or retribution, and in this repression is in complete defeat.

A young man underwent many unusual traumatic experiences during World War II, in which he emerged as the only survivor of his whole battle unit, losing many close friends, some of whom died in his arms. Attempting to put the broken world back together again, he went to medical school and became a very skilled, widely respected doctor. But when a controversy arose in his town over community issues, he found that his old wounds had not completely healed. Cynicism and despair over human nature so overwhelmed him that he refused to be involved in any relationship where antagonism of any kind was possible. The withdrawal was gradual, eventually invading his whole social structure. He retreated from his role as husband and father. His practice deteriorated because of his cavalier treatment of patients, but he pretended not to notice. Eventually he took a position as technician in a hospital, where he could be left alone.

A minister's position is a front-row seat to a parade of bewildering defeats. They come, late at night or early in the morning, their eyes wide and haunting, seeking help. No, not really the restoring kind of help, just food or money or shelter to continue the nonexistence for a time. There have been concert violinists, industrial tycoons, infamous gangsters, former mayors, ship captains and able-bodied seamen, Indian chiefs, and Y.M.C.A. secretaries. In every case, there is a poignant tale of once having had everything, but some horrible distant cosmic injustice moved in, and here is your helpless servant now before you awaiting your pleasure.

They never knew how they hurt me. In every instance I could see myself, for where they had surrendered, I too had partially conceded. Where they had drawn the ice-cold curtain of apathy, I too had in some measure ceased to care. Even at that very moment, while I was turning off my own caring (sometimes to ridicule them behind their backs), I knew enough what I was doing to hurt. Only my method was not to shut the door in their faces with an honest "I don't really care about you" but by a much more sneaky feeding of their neuroses by giving them just what they asked for, including an hour's friendly conversation, and sending them on their way with their words of gratitude in my ears. I was really just playing the same game with myself that they did. It was defeat. The easiest way out. On those rare occasions when I pulled my head out of the sand and looked at my own exposed posterior, I was horrified and humiliated.

But let there be no misunderstanding. I wasn't defeated at their hands. My battle was lost before the doorbell rang. It was lost when I gave up trying to carry my real scale of values into the human arena and put it up for the grabs of acceptance, rejection, or evaluation. And all that came about because of the inward clash of fantasies and aggressions that took the form of a ball of snakes. It would have been better to be hostile, vituperative, violent, defiant, or confessional, or even grief-stricken. I was none of these. Outwardly always proper, inwardly depressed, dismayed with my own scrambled and self-contradictory goals. Outwardly in the world, inwardly in hell.

That's what I mean by defeat. In those unguarded moments when perspective seemed to come, I could see myself joining that procession that came to the door. Riding freights, sleeping in parks, panhandling meals, whimpering for sympathy to every friendly face, but completely insulated from any human encounter. It would be *so* easy, so untroubled.

It would be hard to describe what defeat feels like, for because of its nature it's not supposed to feel at all. It is the thick darkness in which all is lost, so lost that it doesn't matter anymore. In a terrible accident some years ago, a truck demolished a car carrying a woman taking five little girls to a Blue Bird meeting. All were killed. In the banality for which interviewers are so currently famous, a reporter on the scene asked the truck driver, "How do you feel?" "How would you feel," he snorted, "if you had just killed six people?" Then, after a pause, he mumbled, "Come to think of it, I don't feel a goddamned thing."

In a courtroom I watched the murder trial of a young wife who had shot her husband in a momentary, blind fury over his friendliness with the neighbor's daughter. The woman sat impassive through the several days of the ordeal, staring into space and showing no evidence of remorse or sadness. When it was her turn on the stand, the attorney asked whether she was aware that a guilty verdict might well send her to the death chamber. "I know it," she murmured, "and I don't care. I just don't care."

That is the sign of defeat. "I just don't care." It means that a very intensive, demanding, costly, painful battle has been fought for a human soul to breathe free air and react to the world with genuine joy and grief. The battle was lost. The soul has retreated to safe ground. But that ground is in hell.

M O T I F

INSULATION

The metaphor here is that of watching a television drama in the privacy of your home, a casually interested spectator with no possibility of personal involvement. You know very well that the characters to whom you are so physically close have no way of reaching through the electronic separation to encounter you or draw you in. They have no options whatever as far as you're concerned, and you have all the control on your end, in the turn-off switch. What a remarkably opportune thing it is to watch the people on the screen so closely that you can count the wrinkles, see the pores, catch all the nuances, and yet be light-years away! It is a respectable form of mass voyeurism, a way to be a peeping tom completely safe from discovery.

This is the sensation in depression. There hangs an invisible plasticlike screen between the sick man and his world, expressed in his way in apathy. It's a weird thing to live in a world like that, as though the live people who love, interrelate, touch, are all a part of a wide television screen, never directing remarks or concerns personally, never talking directly to, but just passing in front. One is reminded of Emily's discovery in Thornton Wilder's *Our Town*. She returns from death to relive one day of her early childhood. The family life that she had so idealized in her memory turned out to be a shallow pageantry of loved ones, missing enormous opportunities to "open up," involve, include. The point is that Emily was dismayed, but the depressed person almost prefers it that way; the possibility of being personally a part of any interactive situation is so painful that he rejects it. Pathetically, all the while he sees those who are genuinely and unshieldedly involved, he has a wistful longing to be like that, all the time making sure it won't come off.

A woman was murdered in New York in full view of over thirty eyewitnesses, none of whom bothered to come to her rescue or even call the police. The incident was much publicized and caused widespread curiosity and judgmental tongue-clicking, probably because it revealed the insular tendency of our whole collective personality. It is this kind of "What the hell?" detachment that leads to a depersonalized society. In the case of an individual, the insulation stops communication both ways, so that he not only finds it difficult, or unimportant, to love but pays the price of not being able to appreciate in any wholesome sense the love of others for him.

It was my lot, many years ago, to be the only witness at what can only be called a psychic murder. The lady had been taken to the hospital for treatment of a serious heart problem. I knew, as her pastor, that it was emotionally aggravated by the apathy and cruelty of her husband. For years he had lived quite oblivious to her person or problems, quite incapable of noticing or responding to her wifely affection. That very morning she had collapsed on the kitchen floor, much to his disgust. After upbraiding her for neglecting his breakfast, he had stepped over her writing body to go to work. Neighbors found her and called an ambulance; I arrived at the hospital an hour later. In great discomfort, she clung to my hand as she told the story and insisted that I call her husband that we might effect a reconciliation so important to her. He was insolent and resentful on the phone, but grudgingly consented to come. I have lived to regret my action.

He strode in spewing epithets and complaints, taking up the diatribe where it had been interrupted by her attack. He ordered the nurse and me out of the room, which was his right as husband, but I was uneasy and returned in a few minutes. The scene there was one of those horrifying events that always causes dark uneasiness when recalled. He was actually killing her with the words of hostile rejection, storming that she had been totally inadequate and a great detriment to his career. "Besides," he sneered, "I won't be alone when you go. I've got another woman, a *real* woman, not a fake like you!" My lunge to interfere was too late. With a screaming groan of dismay and pain she died. Staying just long enough to get the confirmation from the nurse I had summoned, he had gone with a delighted smirk on his face. In a subsequent interview after the funeral, I could detect no semblance of guilt or even understanding of what he had done.

This is an extreme case, of course, but the difference between that and any other kind of pathological withdrawal is not major. The wife who subtly closes her husband out of her life and thought, but tolerates him around the house as a social necessity, is doing somewhat the same thing, and in that sentence I have described more marriages than statistics can muster. The philandering male who sleeps with two or three different women a month, making convincing love to each, is treating them as objects instead of persons, and has built in a sexual insularity that in the long run will hurt him more than them.

Eventually, it is the interior suffocation that makes depression unbearable. After a while, the individual wants to be able to step into the television-drama situation, but cannot. He sees the sincerity of grief and humor, of love and dismay, of dedication and selflessness, and he begins to wonder if he is under some divine sentence to be one step removed from what's going on in humanity, and the loneliness becomes oppressive. He asks himself, "Why can't I laugh like that?" or, "That person is really willing to give of himself to that cause. Why can't I?"

The difference between the depressive and the truly schizophrenic is again one of degree. The latter, however, has accepted his prison as his world and no longer yearns to get out; he stays in there in happy unaffected isolation. The outside world is no threat at all. It just doesn't matter that much. In fact, it isn't even there. An Army colonel in a veterans hospital in Los Angeles greeted me with a benign smile and a sunny disposition, but when I asked him his name the deepest concentration couldn't produce it. He was out of it, but he was untroubled.

The old saw about the difference between a psychotic and a neurotic applies here. The psychotic, says this quip, believes that two and two make five and he's happy about it. The neurotic, on the other hand, knows quite well that two and two make four, but it worries him! Use the words "schizophrenic" and "depressive," and the description is surprisingly accurate. The depressive knows that there is a world out there, he knows that the dread deadness inside is preventing him from being with it, and he's suffering from claustrophobia. This picture is so real to me that in my blackest hours I even find it difficult to breathe. Once I went fishing with two good friends, hoping all the time that no nosy fish would be so cruel as to get on my line. It might force me into the unwanted action of pulling him in, having to converse lightly with my companions. Both of them would have gone unnoticed by me if they had fallen overboard and sunk like rocks. So I sat there, clutching that miserable rod, suffering to my toes, because, doggone it all, *I like to fish!*

What had brought it on? Fantasy. I told reality that I didn't care for it; I preferred to hope for the unattainable. Result: reality and I had a quarrel and I lost, sentenced to my insulated imprisonment and attacks of demons.

A highly promising young man became a career foreign-service employee of the State Department. After brilliant performance in several countries he was given a consulate of his own in Southeast Asia. But the making of policy decisions became a monstrous threat to him, and he grew insecure about criticism for his mistakes. His formerly neat desk became stacked with unfinished work, untidy with trash. He turned garrulous and insensitive, finally even ignoring directives of high importance from Washington with a shrugging, "To hell with them!" Tragedy was averted by demotion to a job with no executive demands. He works today as an obscure clerk-typist, efficient, detached, and withdrawn. All his former friends are out of contact; there seem to be no new ones.

This is the aspect of depression that the outside world has difficulty understanding. When a person appears apathetic, it is too easy to conclude that not caring is equivalent to not feeling. I can report from inside the tunnel that the caring does go on, but in weirdly frustrated, inverted, self-accusatory, suffocated exasperation.

In this stultification which becomes the dominant aspect of life, one comes to understand a little of Jesus' parable about the rich man and Lazarus the beggar. In this case, the riches symbolize to me the paralysis of fantasy. When the rich man, now in Hades (!), saw that he had missed the whole point of interacting humanity, and that it was Lazarus and not he that was in Abraham's bosom, he wanted to get through to his brothers. But communications had been shut off; it was too late. "If they do not hear Moses and the prophets, neither will they be convinced if some one should rise from the dead." (Luke 16:31.) The stifling wall of death kept him from expressing his real concern. What is worse than feeling that you could indeed be a person of love, but through your own intransigence have severed all means of getting it out of your separated world?

Jesus called it hell.

RESOLUTION OF THE MOTIFS

These are only some of the component parts of depression. They are reviewed here completely in a subjective reference; the sick man is the last one who can give a clinical description of his own illness. So these are not diagnoses, or even an analysis of the symptoms. These pages are one way one man tries to expose

his emotional response to what radio announcers call "circumstances beyond our control."

A very sick spirit once snorted to Jesus, "My name is Legion."
As I write, I am uncomfortably certain that my name is Legion.
There are many of us, but we are not a fellowship; we are more
separated from each other than we are from the rest of the world.
We do not communicate with each other because there is nothing
we have to say; we would probably only intensify the disease in
ourselves. But being Legion doesn't mean that we aren't a notable
segment of man. We're here, and we belong, and the world
needs to know us.

Keith Miller is another one of us, as he tells us in a book,
The Taste of New Wine (Word Books, 1965): "There was no
way I could explain to the people around me what had gone on
and was going on inside my soul, behind the confident mask I
showed to the world. I began to work, because I had a wife whom
I loved very much and two babies I loved deeply. But there
seemed to be no hope, no ultimate purpose, anymore. If there
was a God, the people at the seminary had subtly hinted that I
must have turned away from Him, (or perhaps this was my
imagination). At any rate I felt things closing in on me in the
inner chamber of my life.

"I used to walk down the streets, I remember, and suddenly
would break out in a cold sweat. I thought I might be losing
my mind." (Page 38.)

Since Americans like stories that have a happy ending, I hasten
to assure all that this unusual book turns out that way, making
it rewarding as well as worthwhile reading.

Because, there was a pattern that was for Mr. Miller a
rescue in time of need, it might be threatening and even more
depressing for those of us to whom that particular pattern could
not apply. I am thoroughly convinced that the indisposition
around which this symphony is written is neither simply described nor easily healed, and I will avoid to the end of my life
displaying certainties that may prove to be false and therefore

injuring methods of treatment. Mr. Miller wrote in the very sincere and quite helpful desire to lead some of the rest of us out of hell. In the mysterious catacombs of the complex human soul there is no completely appropriate "how to . . . ." Each one of us has to work out our own salvation with fear and trembling. On these pages will appear only a wondering about the mystery of it all.

But even while we have groveled around in the murk of what has sounded so far to be a thoroughly morbid subject, we see that there are yet certain testimonies of an undeniably positive nature just in the discussing of them from the inside. Take brooding, for instance—a very powerful and effectively demoralizing pursuit. It is a trap, a sump, that also impresses itself on its victim as a kind of purgatory. Animals don't brood; they aren't equipped with that kind of moribund imagination. Therefore, just to brood is to give evidence of a longing to be free from these bonds, to be somebody in the face of the fear of being nobody.

A distraught mother stood at the bedside of her adolescent son who had fallen from a cliff and was only partially conscious. "Don't you see, Doctor," she cried, "he's in great pain? Can't you do something about it?" The physician replied with great tenderness, "At this point, as long as he hurts, he's still alive and fighting to recover. Hard as it is, we've got to see it as a good sign."

Brooding *is* a way of fighting. It is visiting upon the self the hostility and resentments that should be directed outwardly, but at least life is still going on. Though it is meant to be self-destructive, it still maintains a kind of subexistence that always gives room for hope. At this point, as the doctor says, we've got to see it as a good sign. There are times when you just have to settle for the best you have, disagreeable as it is. Once, when it seemed to me that every breath I was drawing was too unendurable to last, the thought occurred to me that at least I was breathing, and I ought not to press for more than that.

Self-deception is also an indication that there is a will to live going on down there somewhere. Crossed up and short-circuited at the main switchboard as it is, yet it is a way of insisting that the world ought to make some attempt to support the fantasies. A person who has put his interests, motives, and dreams on a collision course with each other has at least put something into motion. If he can survive the wreck, he may be able to repair the track and get something more consonant on the road. He may even build a better road than he had before. There is no certainty that it will turn out that way, but there is a reason for hope, even though at that minute there doesn't seem to be much hope in sight. Our own nation's survival of the Civil War is a case in point. More destructive of human life than all other American wars put together, this showdown of the "house divided against itself," this calling a halt at tremendous expense to a national self-deception nearly wiped the whole country from the face of the earth. But there was a profound and almost unpredictable homeostasis beneath the insanity, and when the smoke cleared away the big wound began to heal.

A minister of a large church felt so deeply the need to perpetuate his appearance of being capable, omniscient, and infallible that he impressed himself in a powerful way on the whole community, hurting the sensitive and depersonalizing the church's ministry everywhere. His toppling moment came and in this moment of blinding defeat he realized his irrelevant masquerade. After a prolonged period of shock and adjustment, he set about with much dedication to mend his ways. It is a tribute to his people and his city to say that he is still pastor of that same church, and even though he has to contend daily with the unhappy consequences of his former tactics, he is doing so in a remarkably reconciliatory way. At least he was alive even while he was mistaken and overcompulsive about how things are.

And defeat? It is one of the hardest won, possibly most redemptive times of life. A good friend once said in an offhand manner, "Everybody should have, somewhere in his career, an experience of total defeat. And," he added thoughtfully, "he ought to know what hit him." Probing into his background, I found that he knew what he was talking about; there had been an especially demoralizing incident which he had indeed brought upon himself. But in his case the scars turned out to be banners for a new day.

There you have it. A movement of feeling about depression, a disease of the soul which only too many of us know reluctantly and intimately. It is a condition that comes from weakness, or unhappy susceptibility, or deliberate refusal to be honest or healthy. It is an experience, a condition, of being in hell.

Like hell, in myth or theology of folklore, it is an awesome mystery and an irrefutable reality.

The Depressed Priest
Reads His Breviary

Psalm 42, verse 11:

Why are you cast down, O my soul?
And why are you disquieted within me?

Yes, why?
Is it my fault?
What have I done to deserve this?

Psalm 42, verses 9 and 10:

I say to God, my rock: "Why hast thou forgotten me?
Why go I mourning because of the oppression of the enemy?"
As with a deadly wound in my body, my adversaries taunt me,
while they say to me continually, "Where is your God?"

Let them tease. I don't care anymore. I don't care
where he is; he'd only punish me if he were close. Yet,
I do wonder why, or whether, he has forgotten me.
I don't think he ever really knew me.

Psalm 13, verses 1 and 2:

How long, O Lord?
Wilt thou forget me for ever?
How long wilt thou hide thy face from me?

How long must I bear pain in my soul, and have sorrow in
my heart all the day?

Yes, O Lord, how long?

Oh, hell, I don't even care.

I used to be sunnier, I had a certain lightness of heart.
But it was all a sham.

There is no real happiness, only a hurtful and very
dangerous self-mockery. I shouldn't have abandoned
myself so utterly to that gaiety; I just fell all the harder
into this satanic pit.

Yet, I have tasted joy; I wish I could know it again.

Oh, this pain in my soul! Or rather, my gut. God, how
it hurts! I really am a miserable fragment of half-
humanity.

This isn't like me. How long will it last? This sorrow
in my heart. O merciful God—that does describe it.

Come to think of it, I actually fear the day when the
gloom will lift and I will be exposed as unable to inherit
my wholeness.

Psalm 22, verses 6 to 8:

But I am a worm, and no man;
Scorned by men, and despised by the people.
All who see me mock at me,
They make mouths at me, they wag their heads;
"He committed his cause to the Lord; let him deliver him, let
him rescue him, for he delights in him!"

And I'm supposed to be a religious man! That ought
to be good for a laugh, if laughing didn't hurt so much.

Here at this time of greatest agony in my life, I can't
believe in God. I am actually one of those standing by
and scorning myself for once saying that I had committed my cause to the Lord.

I am so completely, utterly, sheerly, and finally alone!

No other man senses the death in my heart; if he did, the terror would kill him. There just isn't any me, down deep, to respond to God. There's no way a dead walking man like me can relate to holiness. So as far as God is concerned, to me he doesn't exist.

Even if he were real, I'd never be able to communicate with him. So I must go through this valley of the shadow alone.

I don't think I will make it.

Psalm 22, verses 14 and 15:

I am poured out like water,
And all my bones are out of joint; my heart is like wax, it is melted within my breast; my strength is dried up like a potsherd, and my tongue cleaves to my jaws; thou dost lay me in the dust of death.

Poured out like water! Limp, formless, nonbeing. Totally unresponsive to the world except to fall from one vessel to another!

Now I know what death is like. No, this is more than death. At least in death there is peace; I'm sure I'll never know peace again. Maybe I have died. Maybe I've already gone to hell.

Yes, that's it; this is hell!

Am I getting what I deserved? Yes, I know my theological training insisted that that isn't the way it works, but I just can't help feeling that in everything I have done and been, I have betrayed God, and man, and myself.

I guess I also understand a wee bit why people who should know better always sense God's judgment in every misfortune. Hard not to. It serves me right.

But it doesn't make hell any more tolerable. O God! O my God! Why?

Psalm 28, verse 1:

To thee, O Lord, I call; my rock, be not deaf to me, lest, if thou be silent to me, I become like those who go down to the Pit.

When I think of the many people over the years who have come to me for help, with their eyes filled with fear and agony, and lonely distress, and I dismissed them with simple palliatives! I was deaf to their real cry. They went right past me on their way down to the Pit.

But how could I have shared that world; how could I have crawled through those pleading windows with assurance when I didn't have any idea of the terror in them?

Besides, there's room for only one, and only a piece of one at that. Somehow, that's no comfort at all. Great heavens, did I fail to give even a signal of shared suffering to those miserable victims?

Is "shared suffering" what the psalmist is asking of God?

Futile, futile. Nobody can share it.

Psalm 30, verses 6 and 7:

As for me, I said in my prosperity, "I shall never be moved."
By thy favor, O Lord, thou hadst established me as a strong mountain.

I remember saying that.

How could I have been so haughty, so self-satisfied? Will I ever know what bruises I inflicted on the tender unprotected around me?

If I have been so thoroughly insensitive as never even to suspect this hurt; if I have lived so shallowly—God have mercy on my soul!

They used to tell me that some would look at me and take heart—my jolly spirit, my confident demeanor; they thought I had seen into the pitch blackness where they lived and saw something for hope.

Now I live there myself and am hopeless.

It serves me right for thinking I had the clue to life. Man, what a fall! It makes me actually tremble inside when I think of those who now feel they "never shall be moved." O God, O God, save them!

Psalm 31, verses 9 and 10:

Be gracious to me, O Lord, for I am in distress;
My eye is wasted from grief, my soul and my body also. For my life is spent with sorrow, and my years with sighing; my strength fails because of my misery, and my bones waste away.

Well, he had it.

It's like catching a pass on the ten-yard line, and then not having the energy even to try for the end zone. Wasted, spent, failed.

Prayer! What scorn I have for that pious sickener. Just to go through the motions of it right now would nauseate me. It would be hypocrisy of the first order.

Not that I wouldn't appreciate a little nonpersonal attention from on high, like a shifting of that heavy pain from my chest.

But not the face of God! I don't want him poking his accusing, inquiring, reproving face into my life! In fact, I don't want *anybody.* The humiliation and embarrassment of being a nonperson in the presence of someone else's personhood would be even more depressing than ever.

If only God's graciousness would come in a nonthreatening package that doesn't degrade my already degraded self with sticky and embarrassing compassion! If only it came from behind, where I wouldn't see it or know he was around, or didn't think he saw me, and then I felt human again. Then, maybe, I could pray.

Psalm 32, verses 1 and 2:

Blessed is he whose transgression is forgiven,
whose sin is covered.
Blessed is the man to whom the Lord imputes no iniquity, and
in whose spirit there is no deceit.

I can't really tolerate the terminology, but I must admit
that I wish I could be forgiven.

I know I can't. My "sin" is one of continuing self-
deception and deliberate flaunting of the divine promises.

I do know that the man who has come to the position
of authentic honesty with himself and God has a cleans-
ing of his spirit that renews all of life.

But not me. O God, not me!

O dear God, why *not* me? Why can't I wrestle out of
this deathly trap? Why do I have to face every day under
the cruel condemnation of a faceless God who will not
forgive me until I face him, and my grinding, heartless
nonbeing in which I have no face, no soul, no self. To
know God is to be a living person, and I am dead. Every
minute of every day is filled with the pain of empty nonexistence.

O God. O God. Forgive me.

But don't look at me, God—keep your distance! I
warn you, God, there is deceit in my spirit, and it isn't
resolved. I live with it day and night, and this disquali-
fies me.

If you come close, I shall surely die, mortified and
alone.

O God, how I wish you could come close!

Psalm 32, verses 3 and 4:

When I declared not my sin, my body wasted away through
my groaning all day long.

*For day and night thy hand was heavy upon me; my strength
was dried up as by the heat of summer.*

I just can't talk to anybody.

It would disillusion them, and ruin my image.

There are simply no alternatives open to me. I could
never go through with suicide. I must grit my teeth, die
inside, and go through the motions of life as though I
were living.

There's too much at stake; too many lives would be
hurt by any public exposure of the fix I have got myself
into.

It's all my own doing; I have to suffer. I just *must*
endure. If that's the word. It's more like a macabre
pageant; inside I am a constant denial of what I am saying and acting outside.

And the price of it all is this detestable darkness, this
damnable heaviness, this accursed meaninglessness. I
am so completely crushed that if there is one little setback yet to come, another demand, I will just have to die.

I can't go on. I just can't. I can't!

Psalm 32, verse 5:

*I acknowledged my sin to thee, and I did not hide my iniquity;
I said, "I will confess my transgressions to the Lord."
Then thou didst forgive the guilt of my sin.*

I don't believe it.

You just can't do it that way.

Or else the psalmist didn't really suffer. If I really
believed that I could reveal the tragic self-destruction
that has been my main motive in life, the messy splatter
would hurt more innocent bystanders than my insignifi-
cant soul is worth. Their protection is worth more than
all the forgiveness in the world to me.

Now why did I say that? Certainly not because I have

any genuine love. Must be that I am too weary to let
them in on it.

Psalm 32, verses 10 and 11:

*Many are the pangs of the wicked; but steadfast love surrounds
him who trusts in the Lord.*
Be glad in the Lord, and rejoice . . .

Oh, hell!

Psalm 38, verses 5 to 8:

*My wounds grow foul and fester because of my foolishness,
I am utterly bowed down and prostrate; all the day I go about
mourning.*
*For my loins are filled with burning, and there is no soundness
in my flesh.*
*I am utterly spent and crushed; I groan because of the tumult
of my heart.*

I've got to admit it. These fellows who wrote this stuff
so long ago really felt it. No modern literature plows
me up so completely.

Fester is a good word. What there is of me has become
so moribund that there is the smell of rottenness and
decay in my nostrils all the time. I am a walking corpse,
and decomposition has set in.

Once I was alive. Once I acted and reacted and inter-
acted like a living soul. At least I thought I did, and
that's the important thing. But no more.

The stench of what once was healthy, but now is a
vain hope and a ridiculous empty echo, is almost more
than I can stand. In fact, I can't stand it and I don't.

I am already defeated and lie in the dust, thoroughly
devastated. And that tumult in my heart! That pain in
my chest! I awake every morning to terror, to the curse
of another day hung around my neck like the Ancient

Mariner's albatross, a day in which I must go through my charade smelling the decay, and doing more harm to the people in my way.

Yes, if the psalm had ended right there, it could have my name on it.

Psalm 38, verses 9 and 10:

Lord, all my longing is known to thee, my sighing is not hidden from thee.

My heart throbs, my strength fails me; and the light of my eyes—it also has gone from me.

Nonsense! Pious trash.

It isn't known to him; he couldn't possibly understand what an unholy, mortal self-hater goes through. Don't you see, psalmist of old? *I* understand you—you talk my language. But I am not God; I can't help you.

If God *did* understand, he would destroy me mercifully, as a bullet through the suffering brain of a wounded animal.

That would be kindness.

But to make me go through this is cruelty, and I just can't accept that God is cruel.

He just must be "out of it."

Irrelevant.

Uninvolved.

Psalm 38, verses 21 and 22:

Do not forsake me, O Lord! O my God, be not far from me! Make haste to help me, O Lord, my salvation!

Please! Please!

Destroy me quickly, O Lord. Mercifully. Make it look like an accident, as though I were the innocent victim of the circumstances of a violent world.

Don't tease me with hope; I am too far gone to ever

hope again. The exercise would only hurt more, and deep, deep, deep.

Make haste, O God.

O God!

Psalm 40, verses 1 to 3:

I waited patiently for the Lord; he inclined to me and heard my cry.

He drew me up from the desolate pit, out of the miry bog, and set my feet upon a rock, making my steps secure.

He put a new song in my mouth, a song of praise to our God.

Does it really happen?

Yes, I know it does. I have seen it in others.

But not for me. I'm too far gone. I'd never let God that close. I'd never admit what I have to face to do it. I'm a goner.

I know, I just know, that if this mess I've got myself into were magically cleared up, I'd turn around and get into another one.

That's not forgiveness. I'll never be able to sing a new song.

I *wish* I could. I really do.

Psalm 51, verses 1 and 2:

Have mercy on me, O God, according to thy steadfast love;
According to thy abundant mercy blot out my transgressions.
Wash me thoroughly from my iniquity, and cleanse me from my sin!

I can identify with David.

He went into that thing with Bathsheba deliberately deceiving himself, just as I have gone into a hundred places avoiding the realities. He had the whole world going for him, as I had. He thought he could carry it off because he was king, but as it turned out he proved to be a real man; he could come to the point where he was honest with himself.

How would I react to a Nathan? What if someone pointed his finger at my nose, "Thou art the man!" Would I say, "By George, you're right!" Not me. I'd lie out of it.

David didn't lie out of it. He said, "God, I botched the deal. Help me clean up the mess." Wow! That's really living.

Psalm 51, verse 3:

For I know my transgressions, and my sin is ever before me.

And so is mine, but I am a stupid ass. I'd do it again, pushing those stirrings of conscience down.

I have no integrity, none at all.

Now why do I say that? I must have something going for me. It's just that I don't give it any value. I always seem to choose to live in conflict rather than to prostrate myself in front of the altar as he did and make a clean breast of it.

Psalm 51, verses 4 and 5:

Against thee, thee only, have I sinned, and done that which is evil in thy sight, so that thou art justified in thy sentence and blameless in thy judgment.

Behold, I was brought forth in iniquity, and in sin did my mother conceive me.

I suppose that's another way of saying, "I'm only human." But here I can really *feel* the blind alley David is trapped in. To be human, "conceived in sin," imperfect, and yet to have to be responsible to God. That *is* a box. Either you pull in your head so you don't hurt anybody, or you "sin bravely" and then say, "Well, there it is, God. Now what shall we make of it?" The trouble

with me is that I sin as a coward, and am too out of sorts
to do anything with it.

I'm tempted to try it David's way.

No. I'm not that confident.

Psalm 51, verses 6 to 9:

*Behold, thou desirest truth in the inward being; therefore
teach me wisdom in my secret heart.*

*Purge me with hyssop, and I shall be clean; wash me, and I
shall be whiter than snow.*

*Fill me with joy and gladness; let the bones which thou hast
broken rejoice.*

Hide thy face from my sins, and blot out all my iniquities.

Yes, yes, yes! What remarkable words! Truth in the
inward being would do it for me. I just don't want to
face it, to accept a reality in which I can't have what I
have sold my soul to have. It means a real rinsing out
with the purgative. A spiritual and emotional enema.

I notice an arresting difference here between David
and some of the other psalmists. He isn't quite so broken
by his guilt, nor pessimistic about the outcome. He must
have been one of these guys with a head of steam and a
general ability to take the gaff and live with it. His
writings aren't nearly so sensitive as the story of Elijah's
depression on Horeb.

I think I'm more like Elijah than David.

But he recovered, too.

Psalm 51, verse 10:

*Create in me a clean heart, O God, and put a new and right
spirit within me.*

It's too late.

God has nothing to work with in me. I'm just an
empty shell.

Do you suppose David was really honest? He must have been.

Yes, I would really like a new and right spirit.

I wonder if it *is* too late.

Psalm 51, verse 17:

The sacrifice acceptable to God is a broken spirit; a broken and contrite heart, O God, thou wilt not despise.

I certainly have that.

A broken spirit, that is. I'm the guy who was always the life of the party, a real sparkler. But now I'm so morose that I dread talking to anybody. Especially a friend. Strangers aren't so bad; they don't know what I once was, and expect nothing. But friends and intimates! A burden to my soul. I wish I could avoid them.

Is this what is meant by a broken spirit? To make it "acceptable to God," it would have to be a sacrifice. A gift laid out to him on the altar.

Impossible! I couldn't lay my broken spirit out as a gift. It would be an affront to anyone, especially God. All the more so because it is a nongift. From a nonperson.

No. It must mean true humility, a contrite heart. That's my trouble. I'm broken, but not contrite.

In all honesty (a very queer phrase for me to use) I'm not really sorry I'm the kind of person I am—just sorry to be caught in the internal conflict and unable to continue milking my way out of the world without inner surrender.

Maybe earlier, when I had something to surrender, it would have worked, but now there is nothing to give, nothing to sacrifice. I am already the dust and ashes that would be left if the right thing had been burned on the altar. I burned it already, serving and worshiping myself.

That's probably where the book of Psalms, and the whole heritage of faith tunes me out. It really was a deliverance for those whose spirits were wounded, yet were honest enough to make an open show of it before God.

I have the eerie feeling I'm just not that kind. Always a spectator where human honesty was a contender. Have I been condemned from birth to be half a man?

Have I ever been with it? I've just ridden the crest of religious tradition, but down deep have been an isolated, uncaring, uninvolved heathen.

So now I am in the hell I brought upon myself. I can't break out of it because I will always have to live with the person I've been, and I can't be assured that I will ever again be happy with him.

God! If I only could just once make an honest sacrifice!

Contrite? I guess I just don't know the meaning of the word. David did; he was delivered from God's despising. And from his own.

Psalm 77, verses 1 and 2:

I cry aloud to God, aloud to God, that he may hear me.
In the day of trouble I seek the Lord; in the night my hand is stretched out without wearying; my soul refuses to be comforted.

My soul refuses to be comforted, too. Oh damn, why? Is this what they call masochism, rejoicing in suffering? Might I be getting some miserable kind of distorted satisfaction out of berating myself all the time?

I have always been a very protected personality. I have never let anyone see inside, for fear that the truth will repel even those who love me most.

Come to think of it, my whole life has been one of calculated deception, traveling on a too-successful acting ability.

Still and all, my soul refuses to be comforted. It's been bombarded with the fullest riches of assurance any man could have.

Maybe it's a way of crying aloud to God. Maybe he will hear me.

I'm afraid.

Psalm 77, verses 3 and 4:

I think of God, and I moan; I meditate, and my spirit faints. Thou dost hold my eyelids from closing; I am so troubled that I cannot speak.

This fellow was an authentic atheist, just like me. The thought of God either upsets him or keeps him from sleep.

I haven't ever really believed in God. Perhaps it would be more correct to say that I have never let the concept of God pierce my defenses very far.

If there really was a God-man confrontation as the Bible suggests, I would have a wholly different basis for life. Isn't that what I am asking for?

What panic the thought of being alone throws me into! How I avoid ever being left with no one to talk to, no one to deceive, no one to impress! Because when I am with myself, I am with nobody.

Yet how I fear being known too well by somebody whose affection I crave. Seeing the real nonhuman vacuum that I am, he may flee.

That's why I am an atheist. I cannot tolerate staring reality in the face, or being exposed for what I really am, which denies reality.

This is the bag I live in. Am I too old to believe? Is it too late?

I fear so.

Psalm 120:

In my distress I cry to the Lord, that he may answer me: "Deliver me, O Lord, from lying lips, from a deceitful tongue." What shall be given to you? And what more shall be done to you, you deceitful tongue? A warrior's sharp arrows, with glow-

ing coals of the broom tree! Woe is me, that I sojourn in Meshech, that I dwell among the tents of Kedar!

Too long have I had my dwelling among those who hate peace. I am for peace; but when I speak, they are for war!

That's a whole psalm. That guy's in a box, just as I am. I don't know whether the deceitful tongue he refers to is his own or another's. In my case it's my own, but I understand his predicament. He must have burdened his poor family and clan with that mournful song, as I have been trying not to do. I wonder if he ever recovered.

At least he stood within a tradition that accepted tortured spirits as the order of the day; they have a collective corpus of sorrowful acceptance of man's problems.

Perhaps if I lived in such a time I would be less trapped. My trouble is that I am a dishonest man in an insensitive culture. If I ever opened up, I'd be labeled as being out of it (which I am) and carted off somewhere.

He at least could spill his guts out and be heard.

Shall I try it?

Psalm 131:

O Lord, my heart is not lifted up, my eyes are not raised too high; I do not occupy myself with things too great and too marvelous for me. But I have calmed and quieted my soul, like a child quieted at its mother's breast; like a child that is quieted is my soul.

O Israel, hope in the Lord from this time forth and for evermore.

Another complete psalm.

This one answered his problem by just not expecting too much. He's a very lucky man. He deliberately limited his reach to accommodate his grasp, and he's got it made. And he makes it sound that he knew what he was doing all along.

Now why can't I do that? My accursed mind reaches to the skies, and my integrity won't get off the ground.

I'll never again scoff at the simple. At least, they're happy. And honest.

I'm neither.

Psalm 139, verses 1 to 12:

O Lord, thou hast searched me and known me! Thou knowest when I sit down and when I rise up; thou discernest my thoughts from afar. Thou searchest out my path and my lying down, and art acquainted with all my ways.

Even before a word is on my tongue, lo, O Lord, thou knowest it altogether. Thou dost beset me behind and before, and layest thy hand upon me. Such knowledge is too wonderful for me; it is high, I cannot attain it.

Whither shall I go from thy Spirit? Or whither shall I flee from thy presence? If I ascend to heaven, thou art there! If I make my bed in Sheol, thou art there! If I take the wings of the morning and dwell in the uttermost parts of the sea, even there thy hand shall lead me, and thy right hand shall hold me.

If I say, "Let only darkness cover me, and the light about me be night," even the darkness is not dark to thee, the night is bright as the day; for darkness is as light with thee.

There's something uncanny about that. I've read it four times over. The words stay the same, but something happens to me each time.

This poet feels completely exposed (it hurts to think about it), yet understood. There's no way you can deceive God; he's a thousand miles down the road ahead of you.

If I make my bed in Sheol. That's hell, and it's been my dormitory for a while. "Even the darkness is not dark to thee . . ."

He may not think my hurt is as serious as I do.

Which one of us is right?

He may be.

Psalm 73, verses 21 and 22:

*When my soul was embittered, when I was pricked in heart,
I was stupid and ignorant, I was like a beast toward thee.*

Yes. Like a beast, an animal. Like my dog, who can
only look with cocked head and raised ears and understand nothing. Only my look at God is filled with hurt
and doubt, not like my dog's trusting eyes.

Maybe, if there were something more than the beastly

. . .

Psalm 73, verses 23 and 24:

*Nevertheless I am continually with thee; thou dost hold my
right hand. Thou dost guide me with they counsel, and afterward
thou wilt receive me to glory.*

Could it be? Is it possible?
This writer has been in hell. It just doesn't sound like
the usual shallow crappy American folk religion.
He may be my brother.

Psalm 73, verses 25 and 26:

*Whom have I in heaven but thee? And there is nothing upon
earth that I desire besides thee. My flesh and my heart may fail,
but God is the strength of my heart and my portion for ever.*

No.
I don't know. It's all so confusing.
But I have nothing else to lean on. I don't even have
this; I really can't swallow it.
But I'll go on another little bit. If these guys could do
it, tortured as they were, I can. Another blind, meaning-
less, empty little bit.
Yes, I think I can do that, at least.

Looking at Bedrock

Way down, way, way down beneath what we know about ourselves, and even beneath the subconscious, are inherited assumptions. They come from so far back in human experience, and are so deeply ingrained in our modern collective personality, that very few of us ever think about them. But life, and especially its tilt and stability, is built on them; a great deal of what goes on in front of our very eyes is conditioned by what, unseen, lies underneath.

Is there a cure for the diseased self-appreciation we call depression? If it were only a malaise of the body, one could assume there was, and set out to find it by research. Or, if it were entirely an emotional problem, as many reputable scientists think, it could be approached psychiatrically. Both of these are valid conjectures; the healing arts should be encouraged to have at it full tilt. But, testifying as one afflicted, I feel that there is more to be asked, probing into the area of what all of us men, sick and well, think about the meaning of life itself.

Depression is an ontological disease. That means a deep and frightened insecurity about just being alive, a numbing dread of existence. It is a separation from the unspoken immovables that we have to have under us, as though our foot were slipping in the darkness from the mysterious smooth rock we know is there into the formless ooze we know nothing about.

What does one do? I don't really know. I don't know "the way out." What I review here is by no means a description of the path to recovery. But there *are* places to turn one's mind; there are unavoidable affirmations that are far more certain, far more enduring and dependable and underlying the health of the ages than my one, wavering, and fragile life. To study these foundations is much more than a technique to cheer one up. For some of us there are times and occasions when, to stay alive, we *must* unearth the profound, get the feeling of putting our feet firmly on the immutable, await the calming down of our soul motion sickness, and behold ourselves. And maybe, start again.

Strangely enough, though I am the one who has been greatly afflicted, lost my balance and perspective, and hope and desire for any recovery or vital awareness, yet I have no trouble or doubt about where these foundations are the most clearly stated. One doesn't have to be pious, or even any kind of believer, to realize that the Old Testament yet holds the right elementary statements of life and man. Even in the wildest moments of atheistic defiance, or hostile withdrawal, I have known that the fundamental myths of Genesis were more important to me than my sanity.

How come? Honestly, I don't think it has much to do with religion. It's just that in the formative years of my early teens, before any system of logical appraisal had dawned on me, these mythical frameworks of How Things Are got in there, deep. And just like the Sierra Nevada Mountains which dominated the skyline where my memory begins, so have these eternally relevant silent affirmations framed the horizon of my world view. Not just to me, but to most men, and cultures, and orders, and civilizations of the centuries. They've always been there; it is from them that all Western ways and most others get their direction.

Principally, here we look at the five classic foundation myths that comprise the introduction to the Bible, to all religious and secular history as we know it. Found in the first eleven chapters of Genesis, they lay out the dimensions of the arena, and the ground rules in the contest of being. To look at them, to see their gargantuan implications, is to see how man started off, what his makeup consists of, and what keeps him going. Their influence can be seen in almost every sample of literature, philosophy, scientific endeavor, poetic confession, love act, and war cry.

These five are Creation, the Fall, Fratricide, the Death of Cynicism, and the Impossible City.

MOTIF

CREATION (Gen. 1:1 to 2:45)

The purpose for a proclamation of the creation fable at the opening of the book of Genesis is not doctrinal. It doesn't teach a doctrine of God, or even a systematic clarification of the mystery of being. It rather affirms reality itself. The value of having such a story as the lead-off line in the rubrics of human thought is the removal of guilt feelings at the experience of valid living.

This is the most desperately needed of all legends. For life of any kind to flow with integrity and continue in hope, there has to be a cosmogony; this applies to all ages and all levels of sophistication. This is the rubber on the pitcher's mound which supplies the foothold for the stance that enables the throw that starts whatever action there is in a baseball game. Without that firmly rooted, rightly placed cleat there would be general uncertainty as to the orientation of the game and the enforcability of the other rules. Though most games could survive this uncertainty, the more serious ones, such as major league and high-money World Series games could not afford to be ambivalent about the pitcher's rubber. Since most of life is played for keeps, and the way nations and cultures have to know their basic suppositions clearly, the creation story is in existence because we have to have it.

"In the beginning God created the heavens and the earth." The

emotionally important word here is neither "God" nor "created," but "beginning." Though a concept of God is fundamental to self-consciousness, and creation a wonderful question answerer, yet the ongoing process of living is the sensation of a flow, a process, a movement *from* and *to*. The bricks of experience are events separated in time, and memories that make sense are recalls of these events and their chronology.

So the word "beginning," which confirms a deep suspicion that ultimate truth is also part of the flow, brings a deep assurance that human life can identify with the real instead of (or more than) the fantastic. Goodness knows, we have enough to feel guilty about, or insecure over, and we've got to put our foot down somewhere and hope that it isn't on shifting sand. Life can sometimes be clouded by suspicions of unreality, of questions about the nature of existence that suggest we back out of taking ourselves seriously. In many places where the creation myth is not known, commonly held assumptions about life flee rather readily into the ephemeral, the negative, and the downgrading of human importance. There are two kinds of fairy tales: the ones that dramatize and clarify the real, and the ones that divert attention to the utterly fantastic. Creation is the first kind because it is always rubbing our faces in the dirt—and it's pretty substantial, workaday, unavoidable, and earthy dirt at that!

Psychologically, the use of the word "beginning" in the legend is tantamount to the word "home," or "identity," or "security," the words that have a basic element of emotional assurance. In California, the standard question is, Where did you come from? for few adults were born there. Somehow, there is a significance beyond the social nicety in being able to answer with a definite geographic answer: Cairo, Illinois, or Tulsa, Oklahoma, or Council Bluffs, Iowa. Just the saying of the words gives the speaker a foothold in time and space; it establishes him as a person, worthy of continuing in conversation. No one would dream of saying, "I don't know," or "I can't remember." That would be decapitation. Or even worse, "I don't think it matters" would be like saying, "I don't exist. Why the hell did you ask?" *That* would be confessing to essential emasculation. Nosirree, Bob! We always come up with that all-important starting line, that place where we began, because it's just too ding-danged important in the whole scheme of things to overlook.

The cry of the American Negro is a poignantly important one for all humanity, for not only does it ask for something from the present, but it pleads also for something from the past. I recently talked with a twenty-eight-year-old unemployed man in the Watts district of Los Angeles concerning the 1965 disturbances there. He pointed to a passing car. "See that guy?" I saw. "He's a Mex. He got his people. They go back into Indian, Spanish families. He get into trouble, they come get him. They tell him he better straighten up. All the Mexican people of Los Angeles, they gonna be hurt by what he do." He went on to point out other nearby minority groups: White Russians, Bohunks, Italians. Then he said, "But if I go out and torch up [burn] that there Safeway store, or slit a policeman's throat with a razor, I'm just another nigger in trouble. My people jest look sad and cluck for themselves. We don't come from nowhere, we don't belong nowhere, nobody care where we goin'."

A few weeks later a highly educated leader of the Negro community in another city told me a rumor that had been happily received and widely circulated. The rumor said that many of the tribes of western Africa had banded together over the centuries to form a very well-developed civilization, including the invention of writing and high-quality education. But, the story went, when the British slavers discovered the central library, in what is now Nigeria, which had a full record and complete history of an advanced and capable people, they saw to it that every shred of evidence was completely destroyed. They did not want this great source of valuable manpower to ever know its heritage; it might raise them up from the subhuman level that the industry of slavery required. Of course, I have no idea whether there is any substance to the rumor at all. The remarkable point is the intense hunger for the Negro to be numbered among the families of man with a birthright and a respectably documented pedigree of reasoned progress.

Life magazine, in a story about the Child Development Group in Mississippi, reveals that many children in the more poverty-blighted sections of the South do not even know their own names, only nicknames. "Occasionally," says the article, "even the parents had forgotten the child's real name, which was not written down because they did not know how to write." And with an insight only the disinherited would really understand, the writer comments, "It is very hard to see yourself as a whole and important person when you have no name." (September 29, 1967, p. 110.) No wonder the rumor circulated with the same emotional element of assurance that any fundamental myth would. It is part and parcel of the *essence* of affirmation to be found in the story of creation. There *was* a beginning. We have every right to be here.

Another rather pathetic way we unguardedly display our strong need for validation is to be seen in the way we are so easily threatened when the creation myth is analyzed. Certainly a major part of the fundamentalist-liberal conflicts of the past several decades has revolved around the credibility of the first chapter of Genesis. No less a giant in the American scene than William Jennings Bryan proclaimed at least a thousand times that if the earth were not created in exactly the way described in the Bible (by which he meant in six literal twenty-four-hour days), then he, for one, did not want to live. Indeed, his own words were made the more dramatic by his sudden death following the famous Scopes "evolution" trial. The cry of the conservatives was that a change of any kind in the interpretation of the text of Genesis was a denial of its whole validity, and any amateur psychologist is quite certain that this kind of absolutist stand is the indication of monumental insecurity and doubt within. The fundamentalist was genuinely frightened, in every sense of that word, that some trustworthy worldly evidence would pull the rug of creation out from under him and leave him unidentified and an unintended accident in a lonely disapproving world.

Believe me, this is so real even to my liberal spirit that it can get to me. Recently I took my sons to a planetarium where the subject of the show was the origin of the world and life. The distinguished lecturer, a member of the California Academy of Sciences, told us of the most recent theories about the origin of organic life. How very important it is for every person to have his fingernails hooked into some kind of cosmogony! Our teacher told us that life is evidently spontaneous, that when there is a proper combination of climate, elements, a regularly orbiting planet, life is probably sparked off (*sic*) by lightning storms. The evolutionary process, then, produces the higher forms in several million years. Although I was thoroughly enjoying the display, and even thrilled by parts of it, I had to admit that deep down there was a certain element of restlessness, even discomfort, because these theories touched some nerve endings in my soul that had to do with creation. It may have been that the man was so dogmatic that he used phrases without the words "might have been." At any rate, the bothersome motion I felt in the misty floor of my soul was related to the pain all men feel when questions are raised about creation. They touch the darksome suspicion that there wasn't a beginning at all, and that all of what we try so hard to believe to be real is just illusory. No wonder we get defensive!

Accordingly, the very use of the word "myth" in this work will be provocative to many. The word seems to connote the fictional or fantastic as over against the real, and none of us can possibly tolerate the thought that creation is all a fiction. The story of what really took place is too vast for man to grasp; the life-confirming implications of what happened are too important for us to get along without. The only way out of that dilemma is for us to be told the truth in a form we can recognize, and so we have a myth. No generation can survive without myth; it is the only way we converse about the things we know but have no other language for. The helpfulness of a myth will be seen in its simplicity. It needs no explanation, for it is clothed in the kind of language that goes directly to the inner person and ministers to his emotional responses to life. Credibility is of no importance at all; truthfulness and ministry to man are supreme.

"Beginning," then, is the word for our souls. The creation myth affirms it, and now we can live.

"The earth was without form and void, and darkness was upon the face of the deep; and the Spirit of God was moving over the face of the waters."

"Moving." Motion means vitality with purpose. Motion means process. Something is happening, and in this story, the happening, like the American Revolution, puts the ground of freedom and existence under our feet right where we now stand. But motion can also mean unrest, searching for an undiscovered goal, leading to guilt and despair.

We sense this. We know we are clapped in between the two bookends of birth and death, and there is motion and process between the two, but the day-by-day responsibility of being assured that what motion there is is meaningful at times becomes quite a burden. We protest the "busyness" of organized life, and the inability to relax and do just what we want to do, and, on the other hand, appropriate millions of dollars to make sure that our retired and immobilized don't turn into vegetables from sheer inactivity. We are victims of motion, creatures of incessant activity, sinking in the maelstrom of the whirling currents of existence, and all we really want to know is, are we going toward or away from the ground of life?

Here, in the second verse, so soon, appears the element of fear and human loneliness that we all read so easily into the vacant spaces. The earth was without form and void, just as we are. This is a primeval description of the turmoil any man is thrown into when that little hitch of doubt, of loneliness, catches up with him. The narrator has to quickly say in the same sentence that the Spirit of God was there, and in motion.

This is the crack so many of us fall into. We sense that awful formlessness, that frightening void in the darkness, and we fall off at the semicolon. I know of no better description from any kind of literature that states better what happens when well-being drops off, depression comes, and life is terrifying. Formless, void, dark. How remarkable that those myth tellers knew it so vividly, so dramatically! They knew that they had to bring the Spirit of God in quickly in the same sentence lest the story make the wrong point. And the Spirit *is* in motion, and so are we. As the bicycle lies on its side when inert, and mysterious unseen forces prop it upright as it is pedaled down the road, so are we held erect in motion.

It's when the quality of movement is tampered with, or accidentally thrown out of kilter, that very unpredictable complications set in. When the American Negro sang, "I'm trampin', trampin', goin' make heaven my home, Hallelujah!" he was rejoicing as much over the fact that he was in transit as that there was a happy destination. You might be able to talk him out of a traditional picture of heaven without hurting him, but if you ever suggested he was stationary, it would be a blow unto death.

Psychologists and philosophers alike have questioning anticipations of the unforeseen problems humans will find in outer space where formlessness and void darkness are the predominant order of the day, and where all sensation of movement or of having a weighted body is gone. Unless there can be maintained a running, moving relationship with earth by radio and instruments, the isolation may be more than lonely man can bear. Especially as the possibility of travel to other planets looms large, travel that may call for several years of confinement to an apparently static space capsule, those of us who have been assailed by our own intransigence here on earth feel inwardly that it may be too much. It may be that the trip is mechanically successful, but that the living organisms which arrive will be something less than human.

The words "beginning" and "motion" immediately sprang man into being an eschatological creature. That is, he looks forward in life and time with hope and anticipation because he came from somewhere with a feeling of purpose. As the Bible, and other stories of healthy men, developed, all kinds of grandiose dreams about the far end of the road evolved, and this carried us through the grinding centuries of apparently dreary, repetitive monotony. As the old line goes, "I don't know where I'm going, but I'm on my way!" it reflects a certain necessary bounce that may sound a little ridiculous but is very sound philosophical health.

But motion can also make us sick, as anyone who has ridden a boat in choppy waters can testify. It comes, say the experts, from letting the direction of the motion go crosswise with your bodily-psychic expectations. Seasickness comes when the horizon won't stay steady; you're prepared to move forward, even up and down, but *dammit,* the earth ought to stay still. Once, while riding a train, I became so engrossed in reading a good book that I forgot I had switched seats and was riding backward. When I glanced up to rest my eyes, and the landscape was moving in the wrong direction, I was thrown into such a sense of insecurity and threat to my momentary balance that I was upset for almost an hour. It was motion, all right, but momentarily I interpreted it as the wrong motion, and all stability was endangered.

Such is depression. There can be a helpless feeling of being swept in the wrong direction, and the inability to comprehend or correct be so painful that total passivity is the only alternative. Or, under the heading of self-deception, the will to move southerly when life is going easterly may be more than a man can take, like riding two horses at once that decide to go in different directions. A third type, perhaps the worst of all, is the loss of any movement at all, being suspended in midair and going nowhere. Why hope? Why dream? Why even think, when vanity of vanities, all is vanity. Vegetables never had it so good.

The creation story speaks directly to childish, inquisitive, wide-eyed innocent humanity. It reaches into the sheltered and vulnerable parts of our minds, and says "beginning" and "moves" and we are ready to know more. This is a cyclic, constant current ever going on, just as radar is a complete round of checking all points of reference 186,000 times every second. The appearance is a single image on a screen, but the technicians say that it stops and starts all over again that fast. Every second of our existence, these affirmations speak to us, and uphold us, and for some, keep us well.

Here the story begins a very meticulous process of unfolding each stage of creation in orderly manner, each complete scene leading rightly and dramatically to the next. The soul-feeding phrase, affirmed each time, is *"And it was so."* First there is the divine intention, "Let there be light," "Let there be a firmament," "Let the dry land appear," and it is made clear to us that every major development has its reason. But when the crisis is on us, even reason crystal-clear and undebatable isn't enough. That's when we want fact, fact—man—fact. So the Bible says that God wanted it to happen that way, *and it really happened.* It was so.

The constant struggle of the thinking person is to reconcile theory with fact—like trying to bring the two images of the stereopticon slide into focus. When one is off, the whole picture is too blurry to see. Some of us are stronger in one than the other, but all of us have to reckon with both of them all the time. The beauty and the authenticity of this all-important account is that it quickly becomes practical, earthy, real. You can imagine the incredulous looks of the hearers around that campfire of antiquity when the teller said, "And God said . . ." and they gasped "Really?" Then the teacher would nod his head deliberately, "And it was so." Really.

Life is so. From an intention in amorphous infinity, there developed the specifics, the hard, real, visible, demonstrable, experiential fact. That's the life we are cast into, not subject to the designs and whims of our vaporous and occasionally diseased minds, but according to the ground rules of being. We only make ourselves sicker by trying to deny it, or living otherwise; it is up to us to accommodate to creation, not fight it. And in the accommodation, or adjustment, or acceptance, we continue to participate in the drama as it unfolds. That is one of the factors of health.

The next positive flavor in the creation story is not so much a word or phrase, but a tender crescendo, building upward to the creation of man, who appears in this story as the supreme end product. One has the feeling of being in a theater as the scenery is being put in place while the orchestra already plays the overture. There is a beginning, muffled drum roll, and as the lights come up, the fields and forests take their places under the skies and beside the seas. The countryside takes on the vitality of birds and animals, producing an atmosphere of anticipation that builds to an almost unbearable tension. Then, almost at the crash of a cymbal and a royal fanfare of trumpets, the climactic words boom out, "Let us make man in our image!"

This hits us right in the pit of the stomach, like stepping off a train and finding that the mayor, the town band, and the National Guard have been waiting for an hour in the rain just to welcome us home. There are other creation myths from non-Hebraic cultures in which man appears only incidentally, if at all. Most of them, like the Japanese fable of Jinnu, are god-centered or fantastically otherworldly. This story in Genesis is unquestionably the story of man, of you and me, and it rings with an incomprehensible ennoblement, the selfsame influence that comes through to us in a thankful-to-be-alive quality.

It is interesting that Buddhism, for instance, has no creation myth either of the universe or of man. Such a line of thought has no consequence, for ultimate value is found in this faith only in absolute, and therefore, impersonal virtue. Hinduism, with its cyclic entrapment in reincarnated life ending in a depersonalized Nirvana, gives no starting salute to humanity as having any uniqueness apart from the rest of nature. It is true that there is much mental health among devotees of these religions, but history's portrayal shows the Judeo-Christian heritage to have affirmations and goals that are much more man-centered. It's because our first basic assumption is that man is somebody of importance.

Man in general, man in community, man in family, and specifically and especially, you and I. When tomorrow dawns in your life, it will have the purpose of being the context for you and your brothers to carry life another twenty-four hours into the future with a mandate to reflect purpose. Knowing this, or sensing this, or unconsciously enacting it without articulation, makes tomorrow worth trying.

Finally, in this canto, another word is given to us as an encouragement to our spirit. It is the word "dominion," "Let them have *dominion* over the fish of the sea . . . ." Man comes along as the epicenter of creation's motion, making sense out of everything else, being organizer, coordinator, the principal fact. He is, as it were, the local foreman for the absentee boss in the whole project of making earth worthwhile. A secondary responsibility, to be sure, but a big one. Dominion means appointment, ability, adequacy, divine trust. It's the way we were put together.

Depression is the failure of confidence. It is the "I just can't do it" surrender. Chicago police recently found a woman walking in the early-morning fog, clad only in a thin nightgown, and were surprised to find her quite rational. In the patrol car en route to the station, she said, "I got up early, looked in at the children, looked at my messy house, my sick husband, and something just came over me. Everybody's depending on me to hold things together. And I can't. I just can't. So I left." The authorities were further surprised when she refused to go home. "No," she insisted. "I've left for good. I can't go back."

She showed more life than many of us do. She at least took a step out of it. Most of us would have stayed in the clutter but given up inside. More of us, "all sorts and conditions of men," do that. We don't feel up to being fully human, so we don't try. But "dominion," according to this story, is not a quality we cook up inside ourselves through sheer Spartan determination. It is a gift. It is part of our creation, part of our being. To be is to have the heritage. It's not a matter of "I can't." That is a totally irrelevant way to look. It is rather a matter of "I am" and the am-ness is the quality of adequacy, at least to be human, to exist, to stay put in the place we were given, and let the process of creation course through us.

This is the symbolism of sexual reproduction. It matters not how our intentions or self-esteem enter into our mating, the process of fertilization, conception, and pregnancy is an otherness, a given, about our being alive. We don't usually deliberately try to spawn new life—it comes to us in the context of being human and performing the deeds that creation has led us to want to do. So it is with the ability to be. It is a gift, a particular characteristic of our creation, and we don't have to argue with it, or even maintain it. If we see any value anywhere in any man, this myth assures us that we can see that same gift in all its mystery in ourselves. A janitor in the NASA office building in Houston was once asked by a journalist if he ever felt awed by the impressive mental giants he saw every day, the architects of the wondrous technology of outer space. His reply was majestic and appropriate: "They have to go to the bathroom the same way I do." Dominion.

Thus does the foundation stone of creation form a tremendously valuable root of Assumptions for Living. Nearly every person you know, most systems of nations and cultures, and surely the healthy people who surround you, are intimately related to and based on this simple myth and its gift to selfhood. It may not cure your depression to consider it, but it is a step toward awareness to acknowledge it.

MOTIF

THE FALL (Gen. 2:15 to 3:19)

Certainly one of the most delicately told stories of all, this myth has an unsuspected positive slant to it. Even though it be played in a minor key, it is not to be thought of as tragic, but necessarily painful. Surely our generation, which has made such a wide accommodation to adolescence and its necessary rebellion, can see more than most that this is the depiction of the birth of individuality, decision, and the assumption of responsibility.

The Garden of Eden is portrayed as idyllic because no demands are made on man; all his needs are at his fingertips. Strange that this is also the fantasy picture of heaven, the place where you don't have to try harder anymore. But both places, nice as they are, have the one outstanding drawback of offering man no alternatives, no decision-making, no way to exert his own creativity, and so both places, at least in the human psyche, are intolerable. We may not realize that this is the dehumanizing context we put our young people in, or our resentful minorities, or the laboring class, or our national enemies, when we prescribe a world of behavior in which they must stay without impudent question. When you tell your teen-age son that he must *not* associate with the disreputable, or get fresh with girls, or touch liquor or marijuana, you are actually saying, "If you do, it will be the crossing over into a whole new set of strong and bewildering problems that will change our relationship to you and your own relationship to the world and yourself." And if you do know what you're doing to him, you might add with Kipling, "And—which is more—you'll be a Man, my son!"

In a way, this is God's role in the story. It was the first recorded alternative that man was offered. In taking the supposedly morally inferior way, our ancestor asserted once and for all that all of us men were going to work our our personhood by facing our choices and taking the full consequence of our deeds. If it were not so, we would be robots, completely amoral because there would be no choices. The serpent made this very clear to the woman: "You will not die. For Gor knows that when you eat of it your eyes will be opened, and you will be like God, knowing good and evil." And so it was.

One rather wonders if the divine tactic here is much the same as when Jesus told his disciples to tell no one of his messianic nature—a little high-level use of reverse psychology. At any rate, the forbidden fruit was eaten, and the wide difference in natures between God and man, and man and the rest of animal life, was established. The expulsion from the garden was like Freud's birth trauma, an unwanted and resented but necessary and basically wholesome development.

We have said that Eden and heaven are both unacceptable for our kind of humanity because there is no air space there for us to operate as determinative individuals. Yet it is this very incubated separation from vulnerable responsibility that the depressed personality longs for—a place where it is not required to be human or morally directive. Let it then be understood that as long as things are going to be what they are, the interval between Eden and heaven is where we belong, with all its flesh-tearing brambles, sexual embarrassments, and general insecurities. Of course, the depressed victim already knows that what he longs for is unreal and contrary to his own nature, and this story won't help a bit intellectually except to increase the suspicion that we ought to feel guilty. But emotionally, in that it asserts what we all already know, that decisions are always hard, painful, arrogant, and dangerous, we just might make some sense out of the pathos of our trying to avoid what all mankind has to face.

Such is the thrust of this story: we're all in this thing together. It is part of the fabric of being human to resist orderliness and morality, to assert and rebel, and to have to live with it however annoying. Perhaps the fantasy that some men get what they want without getting their wrists slapped eggs us on, and this fantasy is the cause of much of the paranoid brooding seen in some of the psalms as well as other writings, sacred and profane. It just isn't a fair world, other people are getting away with murder while I'm on the short end of the stick, and the sheer inequity of the whole thing disgusts me (so goes the line). But, good brother, says the myth of the Fall to our hearts, that's not only our human heritage, but each one of us gives it a continual run-through every time we move!

It is the Fall that assures us that being human involves a rough road of individuality, rebellion, discovery, taking the consequences, and moving on, a bruised but wiser creature. *That's* the

standard path of life rather than Eden, or Nirvana, or comfortable disengagement. The first-time sea traveler on the decks of
the *Queen Mary* was surprised to note how violently that levia-
than of ships rolled in a heavy sea, and he cringed in fear when a
particularly large wave broke across the bow. An experienced
passenger nearby grinned happily at the same wave, commenting,
"Boy, you should see her ride out a *real* storm!" Same sea, same
ship. One was afraid because he didn't know that rough waters
were usual; the other was secure, for he knew the ship was built
to take it and more. So the myth, built into the basis of being for
the healthy man, tells him that all humanity can be its own worst
enemy, and rather than total oblivion, "You shall not die." It's
the order of things.

Another color in the same reflected spectrum is the heroic survival and creative reorganization of man's life in the wilderness.
Catapulted from the garden, the refugee couple encounter a
whole new kind of existence. But it is not until this takes place
that new life, in the form of children and elementary social
organization, appears on the scene. From the dismal prediction
before that this step would lead to death, the story tells instead
that mankind, even though laden with a sense of guilt and
stained with disobedience, brings into being a new order of
earthy realism. It is in this new order that the things which touch
the nerve endings with some feeling of reward and accomplish-
ment are developed. The guarding angel with the flaming sword
at the east of the Garden of Eden is the very mature realization
that every man should know full well: *there is no turning back.*

This is a most unusual folk myth. It doesn't try to absolve man
from his earthbound imperfections; it doesn't try to put him in
God's place, or exalt any of the desired fancies that a comforting
fairy tale would. It says, in quite simple and dramatic terms, that
man is man and not God, and there's no secret about it. God says,
"Behold, the man has become like one of us, knowing good and
evil; and now, lest he put forth his hand and take also of the
tree of life, and eat, and live for ever . . ." There, that's settled.
There is a definite boundary line between the temporal, finite,

and eternal, infinite. Man definitely has his place. "In the sweat of your face you shall eat bread till you return to the ground, for out of it you were taken; you are dust, and to dust you shall return."

It is this matter-of-fact definition of mortality that comes through as so very important to us. We are dust, of this earth, only temporary. That's the arena of our living, and if we let our wild ideas go beyond mortality, we only hurt ourselves. It is the acceptance of the hard truth, the unapologetic assumption of the human that is the authentically healthy tone of this story. One might tend, after the splendor of the creation chapter, to assume that being related to God so intimately would be like having a rich and generous uncle who would do for us what we ought to do for ourselves. But the story says that we insisted on disinheriting ourselves deliberately, so we might as well make the most of it. It therefore comes as a necessary balance to the creation story to keep the wild exhilaration at being in the "image of" from seducing ourselves into thinking "more highly than we ought to think."

When a man is sitting in a dark corner somewhere, head bowed and spirit feeble, it may help him to realize that he bumped his head on the same ceiling that Adam and Eve did. He assumed too much about the dimensions of life and hoped too wildly and got bruised. The redemptive insight here, hopefully, would be to see that this is where human history began, not ended; here is the incident that brought man to himself, not against himself. So may it be with contemporary man.

MOTIF

FRATRICIDE (Gen. 3:20 to 4:20)

The story of Cain and Abel is a frank and startlingly honest exposure of conflict, self-deception, and the amazing virulence of man's resentment of himself. It comes in the mainstream of the story of man, one of the vital connecting links in the unfolding of the picture of all men. The hippie whom I accosted in the Haight-Ashbury scene in San Francisco protested: "I've got to find my identity, man. It's my thing. Like I gotta know who I am. How am I ever going to get turned on until I find where the handle is?" I marveled at his naïve presumptuousness that by starting at ground zero, overlooking the heard-learned wisdom of the centuries, he could go very far in a short lifetime. One thing was for sure, that if I suggested that part of his identity was to be found in suppressed hostility and fierce violence beyond control, he would have written the whole conversation off as hopeless. His idea was that he and his ilk were the "flower children," the family of love, to whom such a thought would be impossible.

So do we all. From the little old ladies of the sewing circle who don't want to talk about the nastiness of war to the idealistic politician who speaks about making "a better world in which to live," we would all prefer to think that hatred and enmity were passing infections in the human scene that will go away if we shut our eyes.

There are two insights in the Cain-Abel myth for us defensive hardhearted men to catch. The first is the unreasonable strength behind our passionate and fragile insecurity. Scratch the surface of any civilized, loving, intelligent man deep enough to threaten his standing with himself (or God) and he becomes a snarling vicious animal, ready to pick up any nearby rod and kill. Of course, in modern setting we sometimes kill certain people, or we kill faceless principles by subtle means, or we kill ourselves by depression or self-contempt or poisonous guilt. We are not talking about *some* men, we are describing *man*. All men. Wars are just corporate, national methods of exposing and expressing this. A murderous, angry mob is made up of individuals who, when isolated, usually turn out to be meek and somewhat cowardly persons who unhesitatingly attribute the real force of the violence to somebody else.

To know ourselves, we simply *must* gain some sensitivity to what we really are when our guard is down. In the anonymity of a crowded street, the rude jostling for the sidewalk, the survival-of-the-fastest dash for the subway door, the hostile epithet, all come from otherwise courteous, warmhearted people. They just may be being a little more honest and more exposed in their raw humanity when out of view of those who know them. I remember with no little embarrassment the occasion when I nosed out another car at a stop light, nearly running him into the curb, only to be introduced to the same person at the party I was hurrying to! No explanations; it was truly the same me on both occasions, and I had to face that fact within myself.

We of the Western advanced cultures have come to think of ourselves as being more decent to our fellow humans than other younger civilizations tend to be. Yet our chickens are coming home to roost in repeated ways that send us back to Genesis to understand. A haunting, nearly terrifying thought is that we might catch a glimpse of ourselves from the point of view of the American Negro. Almost comic is the surprise of the white community over the strong feeling behind the phrase "Black Power." We may think we've been pretty nice to everybody, but the Negro has a long-suppressed memory of unbelievable indignities on our part that we just couldn't possibly acknowledge. It is a historical fact that until the disestablishment of slavery, the black people were not permitted the legality of marriage, consequently they were bred like cattle, sold as property, and treated as animals. That only starts the story, much of which wasn't much changed after the Civil War. Practically no Negro in the United States today goes though a whole day without some expression of degrading indignity from a white quarter; it varies from physical violence to a scornful look. You didn't think of it that way, did you? Hard to believe, too. Hard, that is, unless you see what the brother versus brother candidness of Genesis is trying to reveal to you about yourself.

We do ourselves no great justice in trying to deny that this is an excruciatingly correct description of us. The second largest nation in the world, India, has in its Gandhi-influenced tradition held the self-image of being nonhostile. There has been no little feeling of superiority by this great country at the warmongering polarity of the cold war. But let a China try to realign a northern boundary, or a Pakistan reassert old claims, or a Portugal rustle its territorial ambitions a little too loudly, and India finds in its system the same readiness to take up arms that all the rest of us have. We're all the same. If we cannot admit to ourselves that we want to murder with the sword, we only fool ourselves into murder with the poisonous tongue, or rivalry in the free-for-all marketplace, or simply the withholding of succor in time of need. The United States, world leader in humane causes, still to this date has not found it convenient to sign the United Nations accord in the condemnation of genocide. Uneasily, and perhaps in brutal honesty, our leaders don't want to burn *that* bridge behind us when there are several peoples in Asia and Africa that might need wiping out someday to preserve our virtue.

The startling development of objective self-discovery is the realization of our hostile nature, how rough it is, and how necessary to our total personality it has become. Cain was caught with his crops down, and in what statesmen might respectably label "enlightened self-interest" he fought his way out at any price, including his brother's life. That's you, brother, and your society.

So what's to be done about it? We're all vicious, selfish animals underneath. Shall we just give way to our natural inclinations, and live in the open honesty of a violent society? Lenin, Trotsky, Stalin, said yes to this, and their wisdom about human nature at that moment was greater than that of the bland world of that day. "Che" Guevara died in the Bolivian jungle advocating it, and so must have died happy. Some of the extreme advocates of the Black Power cause feel they are more correctly reflecting their humanity by advocating it, and again they may have a certain flavor of realism. But all of these dream of a society in which other values are exposed and exalted by the violence, so a pure doctrine of raw human hatred always awaits other traits in man to be complete.

Here the story does not let us down, for it is the second major insight that whenever man is exposed to himself he simply has to react with a socially responsible conscience. Unsurpassable in its poignancy and unmistakable in its meaning is the passage:

"Then the Lord said to Cain, 'Where is Abel your brother?' He said, 'I do not know; am I my brother's keeper?' And the Lord said, 'What have you done? The voice of your brother's blood is crying to me from the ground.'"

The story tells us that no man kills without a backlash of grief for what he has discovered about himself in the killing, that he responds to this unanticipated voice within himself with denial, or evasion, or escape, or hostility, or depression, or insanity, or any of hundreds of kinds of pathological inhumanities. But no matter what he does, the whole community, the whole creation is hurt by the spilled blood which cries its own eloquent commentary on an order of Godlike creatures that would be so idolatrous as to destroy what God has made.

This is the beauty of this pathetic narrative. When the horror has happened, all has not been said. Raw, dirty, blind, selfish passion has been unleashed like a powerful lightning bolt, but in the aftermath a quiet epitaph reads, "Both God and man have been hurt, and both need each other." So Cain is cursed, and branded, and sent into a far country, just as we are saddened, or embittered, or reconciled, or forgiven and continue on, but never as it was before. We are marked with a new realization and a new bewilderment, and it will color our interpretation of everything that happens from now on.

The careful man who prowls around in his subconscious to find out why he does what he does will not come up with very many satisfactory answers. But if he can accept the seeing of himself as a creature who will demand that others pay dearly for his being, but not without leaving significant pieces of himself with everyone he has wronged, he will indeed be a fortunate man. Of course, he will have to learn to bear the rather oppressive burden of guilt and handle it wisely. For he will never escape guilt; he will have to arrange his reality-adjustment meachanisms to make

it more a vaccination than an infection. Cain was marked for
life, but he did carry on, and is found in the genealogy of the
patriarchs; he is our father, says the myth. He is one of the de-
scriptions of humanity, says the translation.

We live in a day, as all days are, in which revolution is a
method of change. Indeed, most of us are citizens of a country
brought into existence by revolution. This presents a major hard-
ship to our sense of ethics, as the use of violence to gain any ends
at all is basically offensive to our ideas of good and evil. At least
a dozen nations have come into being since World War II by
violent overthrow of status quos, and another dozen have changed
regimes this way. Our part has been to stand awkwardly aside,
wringing our hands and deploring the necessity. Occasionally we
approve and applaud, as in the Dominican Republic; occasionally
we deplore and judge, as in Cuba. We have decided to make no
outright judgment on the means of revolution itself, preferring
to reserve our opinion on whether it turns out for us or against us.

This is an important point in dynamic psychology and theology
as well as history. Just what *do* we do with revolution anyway?
Well, good friends, the morality of revolution is a macrocosmic
picture of an inner man, committed unconsciously to any method
at all that will preserve, protect, or reform. All societies are the
same, and all countries are really, existentially, committed to
revolution as the only way to bring about the needed social
change in a poor country, or protect the situation as is, for a rich
country. In open recognition of the right of any country
to resort to its own means to accomplish its own ends, even
the Christian leaders have come to a more favorable disposition
to accept the authenticity of revolution. In point of fact, as we
study the entrenched and abysmally tyrannical governments of
many underdeveloped nations, we find ourselves hoping that it
will take place the sooner the better in many situations, as the
only possible way of effecting human justice fast enough to keep
up with a dramatically fast-moving world. A world and a society
that can bring itself to look at revolution without supermoral

disdain, and without guilt or cynicism, but see it as a fact of human history, will be better emotionally equipped to deal with its consequences responsibly and perhaps even redemptively.

It is a picture of ourselves. Psychiatry has tried valiantly to pull the picture into better perspective by using the word "aggressiveness" without a negative cast. It refers to a vital expression of the desire to live and stay alive in comprehensive contact with the right things. Because it is an outward thrust, aggressiveness can come out in hostile chunks, or in punitive violence, or in more creative and helpful means, but when it comes, it is the validation that genuine life is behind it

So when we find ourselves gripped by forces within us that we do not understand and can't seem to control, and resort to means that we didn't think we ever could employ, we are the sons of Cain. A proper assessment of this is not just the shrug of the shoulder and a disclaimer of any wrong; that's not what happened to Cain. It is, rather, the mature preparation to live in the next and unpredictable stage that will be ushered in by the aggression, to live in it with an appropriate acceptance of the damage and a reconciliation to the liabilities of it. Cain started a new life elsewhere with an indelible mark on his life and a new insight into humanity, and we are the children of that life. But in all fairness to that new life, we cannot drag the obsolete guilt of the past along with us and let it limit or downgrade our humanity. We go ahead.

Personal depression is frequently marked by a self-despising that leads to nonsensical self-punishment. We don't see a whit of this in Cain. In spite of being the villain in an old story, he was a healthy man, and as such is a key to our being healthy men. A mature, fairly well self-disciplined man took his wife on a long automobile trip. On a stretch of narrow highway, he became so enraged at the discourteous driver of the car in front of him that he lost his temper and tried to crowd him off the road. It proved to be a very unwise effort, causing a major accident involving yet another car, and several serious injuries. Long afterward he said, "For several days I was so ashamed of myself that I couldn't speak to anyone. The constant parade of insurance adjusters, police interrogators, court appearances, seemed more than I could possibly stand, and I thought it was the end of everything. Then it came to me that there was nothing else to do but to take my medicine and do my very best."

He was lucky that it "came to him." It *was* the only thing to do, and it was an exceedingly valuable lesson for him and those who were influenced by him. One of the finest moments in U.S. history from the standpoint of emotional maturity came when President John F. Kennedy, white-lipped and somber, appeared before television to acknowledge to millions that the invasion of the Bay of Pigs in Cuba was his misjudgment and his responsibility. It was such an obviously right thing for him to do and for his nation that many were strengthened to be more honest with themselves because of it. Since he could live with himself in the light of an international disaster, many of us took courage to go on living with ourselves and our own disasters. All of us, J.F.K. and the whole host, bore a Cain-like mark on our spirits but stayed in our places to do what we must.

These revelations, in history and myth, provide symbolic guideposts we cannot afford to overlook. Everyone of them is a dramatic enactment of our own human dilemmas projected on timeless screens and amplified to the corners of the earth. And in those moments of acute and unexpected loneliness, when in a dark blind alley and we don't know what to make of life, they come through in remarkable clarity—if, that is, we are so fortunate as to have known of them.

That, simply put, is the reason for replaying the Assumptions for Living from so far back; they turn out to be quite contemporary.

M O T I F

THE DEATH OF CYNICISM (Gen. 6:1 to 9:27)

The story of Noah and the ark might more positively be called the death of *divine* cynicism. It explores the terribly demanding question of whether man has any right at all to survive when he takes his own creation so lightly, or so destructively, that even God feels frustrated. It quite daringly rehearses every aspect of divine despair, yet ends with a covenant to go on trying.

"The Lord saw that the wickedness of man was great in the earth, and that every imagination of the thoughts of his heart was only evil continually. And the Lord was sorry that he had made man on the earth, and it grieved him to his heart."

It is really quite remarkable that such an eloquent picture of a despairing God comes from such antiquity. Obviously, those who told this greatest of narratives were quite sensitive, deeply involved, unusually honest men. How else could such a tragic and pathetic picture of man be portrayed, than to say that God was disappointed? How more touching to unfold the darkness of man's grief at himself than to indicate so simply and touchingly that God also wept? Here is reflected the symbolic cosmic grief that all mankind cannot hold back at the sadness of imperfect humanity. How could you help being cynical? So does a significant part of every community surrender to cynicism, caustic and disillusioned despair, and it's a story always being repeated.

It is, however, not total despair. "But Noah found favor in the eyes of the Lord." Despair as such is not always fatal; one little micro-spark glimmer of hope can, like a feeble candle in a universe of darkness, hold its own. Modern cynicism isn't all bad; even Jean-Paul Sartre finds himself (frequently to his own surprise) involved in movements of French social reform. Jeremiah could call out his dreary forebodings from the bottom of the pit, yet emerge to invest in real estate as an affirmation that a higher order triumphs over the stale stench of human defeat.

The story of Noah rises to a rather emotionally stirring height at the relationship of hope and promise in the colorful construction orders on the ark. Both God and Noah are investing everything in this one shaky venture, but God's risk is thousands of times greater than Noah's. God, in heavyhearted despair that the sacred beauty of life has been so profanely abused by his honored guests, bets the whole destiny of his intentions on this one man, this one fragile fallible possibility. He is hoping that he can retain the individual freedom of his creature yet preserve in him the divine dignity for which he longs. So the crackpot plan proceeds and the vessel is built. He wants more than just to save man; he yearns for a new Man.

A new Man! How quickly in the development of things did man sicken at his old self! This story, in differing forms, is well over five thousand years old. Far back in what we would call the dawn of recorded history, our collective and representative spirits fell and we wished we were different.

The Old Man was nearly intolerable; we just didn't want to go on that way. But we *did* go on. Noah survived the flood, only to pick up the old habits, but the rainbow was given to us as a symbol that both God and man have decided to keep hoping.

Keep dreaming of that new Man! That's why this passage can be called the death of cynicism—*total* cynicism, that is. It will also help us to maintain our emotional balance if we see that the story of Noah's ark is a reminder to Twentieth-Century Man that he may not stand, as he so easily tends to suspect, at the *latter* end of history, but possibly *well toward the beginning!* Obviously both God and Noah felt that the old ways were pretty old, that there was nothing new under the sun, that history had pretty well run its course, and it just hadn't worked out. Tired and discouraged, God (as the storytellers saw him) was just about ready to wipe out the whole project.

But after the first executive decision to abort—or "scrub the mission," as NASA would call it—there comes a reconsideration. Noah will be saved on the running chance that a new kind of man may yet develop. Even God, then, reverses his field from regarding the situation as terminal to screwing up his spirits to start again. God can never stop dreaming of a new Man.

It is this wild, irrepressible, enticing dream, bubbling up from the centuries of way back that comes through in this myth as the golden trumpets for us today. The logic is simple: if the old man is unsatisfactory, if the record shows over and over and over again that human history stumbles blindly into dehumanization and degradation, what's the purpose of it all? Why not give up? But to the logic is added the intuitive hunch that there's more to man than he's been so far, and up ahead with God's help a new Man cometh.

So too is this a personal experience where dread of being, hard and heavy, is still not enough to quench a little, fighting dream that makes it worth the effort to start all over again. So the flood of despair and the ark of hope, and we can't help dreaming of a new self inwardly and a new Man historically.

How wild those dreams can get, when the spirit is strengthened to imagine without fear! The myth speaks across the millennia to us to keep up the dream, to uncork our bottled-up optimism, and even fill in the details in our mind's eye. So let's have at it!

Speaking of Dag Hammarskjöld, Henry P. Van Dusen told a gathering of churchmen, "He was truly a Renaissance Man." It was the Secretary-General's reveling in the aesthetics, his gleeful rolling on the grass of a culture that spoke of its own neo-human-ity that brought this honorary title. Dr. Van Dusen told of the earnest openness, in which Dag found as much fulfillment in absorbing the hues of a Rembrandt, or hearing the confluent sonority of Beethoven, as he did in resolving international ten-sions. The remark was gracious and made its effect in proper sophisticated sentimentality.

But why do we have to reach into the pre-Einsteinian age to find a descriptive comparison? Mayhap Hammarskjöld is indeed a human anachronism, a holdover in modern clothes. But, darn it all, he *was* a man rooted in something, whose life caressed the international spirit with a startling tenderness.

Whatever our different philosophies of history, most scholars will occasionally concur in a typology, such as "Medieval Man" or "Renaissance Man." The kaleidoscope of cumulative culture, assiduous accident, and provoked progress seems to bring together, every few eras—give or take a century—a convergence of knowledge, institutions, political climates, multiphasic theologies, and transcendental intentions that work together in defining humanity in a new and refreshing way. These are the times that produce a universal self-consciousness. It is as though we were all afloat on a raft in mid-ocean and an unusual crest lifts us up to a momentary view of horizon and stars, long enough to adjust the sextant and calibrate the compass before losing the whole inclusive perspective.

Of course the whole thing could be delusory, unreal. We think we see something of long-range significance in the polarities of our time—the *élan vital* of our sexual imagery vis-à-vis the frightened bleatings of the threatened comfortable—the prognathic liberalism of government and the social sciences over against our international intransigence. We bow with hushed reverence before the altars of a technology that has put us in instantaneous touch with almost everybody else in Manhattan, Moscow, and Mars, and vaguely wish we knew the real substance of communication. We may indeed be in the trough instead of on top. There may be a new Man in prospect, but not in our day or on our continent or in our "civilization." Willis B. Glover can toss out Harvey Cox's nomination of John Kennedy as "Twentieth-Century Man" by noting that his acceptance of Roman Catholic orthodoxy makes him atypical. So be it; perhaps there are too many disqualifying factors in the air just now. And yet, we've grown accustomed to the thought that, well, *something* is going on that resembles the creative turmoil of previous times. Something is being said in contemporary art, music, architecture, literature, those pressure gauges on the instrument board of history whose needles have been trustworthy indicators of performance in the power plant. Something is being said in the very way major traditional institutions have volunteered to clean out their attics;

the Vatican cheerfully announces that what had for years been represented as reinforced concrete turned out to be reformable plastic, and North Korea proclaims that it will use its own non-Chinese revised standard version of the holy Manifesto. Something is going on in the major shifts of current under the general headings of health (prolongation of meaningless life, therapeutic abortion, euthanasia, birth prevention), of education (indoctrination for predictable obedience, or freedom for innovative disruption), of politics (dare we trust a new nation to have to go through the same destructive chaos it took us three centuries to accomplish to govern themselves?), in war (?), and on and on. Well, at least it is respectable to say that there *could* be a new Man coming on. There could be.

All of us sidewalk superintendents stand around the excavation and imagine different things that will go into the construction. It depends on our interest; some will think of plumbing and heating, others of elevators and penthouses, still others of gardens and the color of tile around the urinals. This writer, looking at the possibility of a new Man, does his musing in the field of the things that make for trust and soul-health and faith, because as an injured man he needs to look there. As for the subjects of international solutions or economic ambiguities, or interracial resolutions, I plead no contest. That doesn't mean not guilty, that my field of interest is not involved; it just says that for this hearing I have no business biting off more than you and I can chew.

If the way it has always gone before has any validity in telling us how it will go again, religion is still in the picture. Men somehow seem to evaluate their humanity best when systematically reconsidering their god. This sometimes results in building foundations under the contemporary, making the "ortho" even more "doxy" and the "status" more "quo," as in Medieval Man. Or it may go the other way and "clast" the icons, as in the Reformation and the ancient Areopagus. But it always enters the scene—religion, that is—as a chart in the pilot's cabin, or a charter for a movement. When man gets ordered and organized to where he can direct his destiny and channel his fears, he becomes Man.

When he starts releasing the courage and sensing the security to reorder and even negate his god, he again becomes Man. The question is, Are we there yet?

We can hope for it, anyway. It will be history that passes the judgment, and if we're wrong, it won't affect our Social Security benefits. If we're right, there probably won't be a proportionate increase in salary. So let's have at it. Let's talk as though there is indeed an emergent new Man, a twentieth-century reaper of the harvest sowed since the decline of the Renaissance, a new sense of the relevance of humanity to the universe, an era-end inventory that lists impressive assets.

We get a running start in the religious consideration by simply preparing a contemporary lexicon. To understand the language of the day we have to retire quite a few words to the shelf and pick up the ones in current use for the same meanings. Modern man has no use for the word "holy"; put "meaningful" in its place. Throw out "heaven" or "righteousness" and substitute "secure." In the place of "sin" put "anxiety," and for "forgive" say "resolve" or "integrate." "Ethical" is more correctly said "relational," and "to obey" is now "to react." For "faith" use "psychic health"; for "hope," "realism"; and for the Biblical concept of *agapē*, "love." Concerned men of today are giving substantial interest to the word "justice."

Once started, this diction can be continued fairly easily. "Worship" as a word goes out of use, but its practice remains, so we call it "demonstration" or "expression." We don't call them "hymns" anymore, but the air is full of "freedom songs," "folk music," "protest songs," and even "Muzak." Of course the actual events of piety, trust, commitment, searching for the tokens of existence, and a rationale of relationships that make living as unique individuals tolerable haven't changed nearly so much as the vocabulary. The word "prayer" won't get much mileage in the Village or the stockyards, or even in Tokyo, but see what a mossy mystique we have already planted around "meditation" and "dialogue," those grand avenues of becoming!

So long as existence continues to be linear, so long as we are still trapped within the dimensions of time and space, so long as our being remains principally organic, the basic setting-up exercises of getting our transcendent minds to operate within our mattered bodies seem to follow the same general patterns. The conversations we give greatest importance to today, given through the spoken and visual arts, are just as religion-oriented as the pyramidal petroglyphs. Shaw, Dylan Thomas, Ernest Hemingway, Camus, Albee, and the rest are grand scribes and high priests. Religion is their obsession—that is, a coming to terms of some kind with the being of man of any kind. So, as in times before, the new Man is assembling his theological marbles to restart the same old game with hopefully new tactics.

Evidently the classic forms and institutions of religion are in for major overhauling. It's just as well; let them go. They have served their purpose well, giving the unthinking a place of refuge and the rebel a cause to fight. They have given a foothold for mankind climbing up the cliff of time to find himself, and a foothold is a thing to leave behind now, and to remember gratefully later. Judaism, Christianity, Islam, Buddhism, Hinduism, and the incantations of the cults and rationalizations of the intelligentsia have joined forces to help us arise on the morrow with a sense of belonging. Now to enter into this heritage at its fullest is the Grand and Glorious Possibility.

The cry "God is dead!" is the landmark of a new maturity. Not that whether he really is matters much, or that even a small number of us understand what the crier is trying to say. The boon is that it can even be said in our day and there be any interest at all in its saying. That we can so lightly discuss what has been an intransigent blasphemy is remarkable, that we *do* discuss it with diverse levels of understanding is a long-hoped-for miracle. It puts a blue-green strain on the imagination to concoct any other headline that would get such enthusiastic coverage: "Einstein Was Wrong!" "Queen Elizabeth Joins Communist Party!" "Congo Has Highest Living Standard in the World!" There is just the slightest element of predictability in each of these that puts them in a different class of credibility. The "death of God," tossed over the shoulder casually by the philosophers at their workbench, becomes the working motto of those who privately thought they were rejects from humanity for suspecting it all the time.

It doesn't matter what it means, or that it ever means anything. It has been said, and since the crowds stood in the bleachers and either cheered or booed, it was the equivalent of a grand-slam homer for *somebody's* side, and everybody was involved. That it was raised by those within the church who are pressing for a man-centered, humanity-emancipating direction in religion will eventually get across to the world. The modern prophets may become or at least inspire a Thomas Aquinas for the new Man. Obviously, the new *Summa Theologica* cannot be written in a cloistered Dominican retreat; it will have to smell of the garbage-strewn alleys of urban decay, resound with the shouted obscenities of forced open housing, systematize the hostilities of the deprived, and justify the ambiguities of international hypocrisy.

The new Man's religion will not be centered on God, but on the undiscovered reality of man. Jesus eloquently pleaded for this long ago, and Bertrand Russell and Karl Marx gave more recent assists. It will not be so concerned with "the nature of . . ." but being a part in "the process of . . . ." In the place of eternal security, its goals will be societal integrity, and the former mysteries of death and judgment will be replaced by the more awesome mysteries of awareness and human sensitivity to love and justice. The historical virtues of service and sacrifice will be strictly "oldsville," and in their place will come the goals of interpersonal authenticity and organized acceptance. But withal, the basic goings-on are the same, the motives and commitments and morals are on the same stage with different costumes and lyrics, but it's the same plot.

The "sexual revolution" is another landmark of religious development. Just take the wire brush of objectivity and scrub away the encrusted erotica, the institutional cheesecake, look down into the illumination and disillusionment of lonely humanity seeking its mirrored confirmations, and in that you will discover again the pursuit of the unknown in human exchange, you have upturned religion. That which is taking place today is not so much the decay of morals, or the denying of an ethical heritage, but a reordering of priorities in the quest for self. It was not really man himself that changed, it was the context of circumstances, the evolving of an economy in which we had uncluttered sexual access to the heretofore unattainable, and we're hard at it like cattle in a field of alfalfa. We're the same bovines we were before the farmer's son left the gate open, but the situation is different, and we are expressing our cattle-ness now as we always wanted to do before. True, more of us will die of the bloat than we would before, but we can't chalk our previous good health up to righteousness.

Sex is a religious subject because it involves the unplumbed possibilities of humans relating in a contributing interaction. It is religious because it has all the probabilities of revealing to us a new dimension of our humanity. It is religious because it is a possible screen behind which we can hide from even knowing ourselves. It is religious because it involves the social situation of more than one human will making parallel volitional choices in tandem. And, it is religious because it is always a quest for release from an enslaving drive we can describe but not fully understand.

The new Man will be so free from unreasoned inhibitions that he will acknowledge the religious dimensions, that is, the life-ennobling aspects of sex. Evidently a preliminary stage in this (as the Black Plague was to Medieval Man) involves a tumultuous reordering of traditional domesticity. The institutions of marriage and family, already pulled into many new arenas of both victory and defeat, yet have many crucible-type refinements to go through. But knowing that whenever a new Man appears a new humanity has been born gives promise that not all the dire cries and hand-wringing laments are fully justified. We've always admitted the truth of the garden story, that man's mind and man's soul don't always travel together happily, and in like manner we still trust, religionist, humanist, and scorner alike, that the cove-

nant of the rainbow is yet in force. Sex, now in danger of losing
its appeal because of its commonness, will prove to be indispens-
able and will appear as it is already beginning to appear on the
new altar in the new temple.

The specter of nuclear hostility is also a religious subject, and
however it is resolved or controlled will be the new Man's faith
in action. The shielded red button on somebody's desk, somewhere in the maze of Pentagon-Kremlin-Celestial City-Gallic bu-
reaucratic hiddenness, is the most dramatic opportunity for a man
to play God. The old myth of Satan with his pointed tail and
tined fork isn't to inept after all; he still must have his boots
licked lest we die. We muse about the tragic psychosis that drives
a Lee Harvey Oswald to an upper-story window, or a host of
other nuts to hiding places from which to kill, and we admit that,
in the last analysis, what a man does is his own guidance from
anywhere, and that could only be a religious problem. Then we
think of that button. And we know that all the safeguards of international control, war-review boards, and restrictions on chiefs
of all staff still can't account for one dizzy moment on the part
of one psychoneurotic with a big, powerful, available, muscular
THUMB. If only we really believed in prayer! What else is
there?

It becomes a religious problem because our own technology is
forcing us to be dependable or die. We have eliminated the buffer
time between thought and deed, and made the deed to be possibly omnipotent. The only access we have to that uncontrollable
little link of whim or decision or impulse or rage is to depend on
that particular powerfully-thumbed man. And since we don't
know him very well, we have to jack up the whole standard to a
place where it is man*kind* that is trustworthy. That happens to
be beyond everything we know now, unless we mechanize all
men and destroy humanity, or ennoble all men. And that's
religion.

Even the traditional sellout is religious. That is, to say: "What
the hell, let's not get all balled up on a subject we can't fix any-

way. If we die, we die; why all the anxiety?" As a matter of fact, that's where we came in in the first place, anticipating the certainty of death instead of trying to ward it off. While we contemplated the whole meaning of *that*—*voilà*, religion!

This may be the focal point around which man will have to become the new Man, or be no man at all. He may have to come to such an honest appraisal of what he really is when there is no room for deception that he knows how to be trusted. There are indications that this very thing may be in the air. Turn first to the major religious communities and listen in on the conversations going on within each household. The significance of Vatican II goes far beyond the details of nearby reform. What has undoubtedly been the world's most inertia-bound movement, locked in the rusty chains of its own institutional clumsiness, can shrug off the chains like wet spaghetti when the cause of man is up for grabs, *mirabile dictu!* True, the evidence of monumental change is yet meager, but one gets the feeling of confidence that in the fearsome nightmare of man fighting for the breath of cosmic recognition, the Roman Catholic Church really is on his side.

Protestantism is not quite so tidy, nor so profound, but it also seems to have the capacity to recover from a historical onset of hardening of the attitudes. The upsetting honesty with which the World Council of Churches is looking at the requirements of peace, the merciless probing of the theologians into the actual components of truth, the dropping of traditional divisiveness (slowly), all militate against the image of institutional religion as a storage vault for discarded ideas. World Judaism has by and large been the cutting edge of ethical insistence and may even sacrifice its cultic paranoia to rise to the occasion.

But perhaps the most significant developments are taking place among those men who with immense dedication are organizing the inferences of life outside the walls of organized religion. That men of stature can stay on the upper point of power pyramids and avoid corruption on the one hand and cynicism on the other

is difficult to understand, but it is happening. It is a lonely kind
of religion, that, but it is a religion, and it is claiming more cere-
monial sacrifices than Chichén Itzá ever did. It may be true that
the run of politicians and public servants in both hemispheres is
mediocre, and generously sprinkled with demons. But it also
has to be true that scattered among the crowd is a small minority
who genuinely do put their very best on the chopping block for
us, who really do struggle for the exaltation of the truly human,
and want no other reward than for mankind to have its day in
court. Here, the so-called Iron Curtain is not the dividing line
between the white hats and the black hats. I have met spiritually
sensitive, dedicated humanists carrying party banners in Moscow's Red Square, marching to Montgomery, and plunking for
Wallace!

There *is* an emergent faith rumbling in the wings. Whether it
beats disaster to the too-dramatic finish line can't be predicted,
but it can be hoped. And there is no other way to hope, so we
might as well go full throttle. That there's something to be hoped
for comes through in living color in the very nihilistic utterances
that seem to be trying to say the opposite. Some of the disjointed
defiances sung over strummed strings in Washington Square have
essentially the same content as a high school valedictory in all
its corny clichés, and both of these are related to the screams at
demonstrating blacks from secluded windows in a Chicago sub-
urb, found rephrased in last Sunday's sermon. We're all crying
for a reconsecrated humanity, mourning its lost or never-born
virtues, wallowing in the sewage of disillusionment, yet *we cry*.
Our formulas of recovery may be vastly different, our picture of
heaven a direct contradiction of our neighbor's, but our protesta-
tions at least come out, at least are voiced, at least are flung to
be heard by *somebody*.

Ah, but this new faith, this new song to be sung, with its minor
modes and its incomplete themes and its atonal dissonance, has
a demanding movement, a hypnotic "beat" that echoes the vitality of our vitamin-enriched, leisure-bedecked, anxiety-pressured

lives. Its thought forms and vocabulary will undoubtedly permeate the streets, so that its liturgies will be the frameworks of all secular concepts and its words the lingua franca of the back rooms. That's the way it developed before, and in spite of our liking to think we are emancipated from the tyrannies of religion and superstition, we seem to be following the very selfsame trends in new dress. If you can't lick 'em, might as well help make policy with 'em.

Religion gives answers and channels of public expression to the imponderable tensions and otherwise unresolvable distortions of our own personhood. There seems to be little doubt that the demographic explosion and the computerized factor of administrative relationships are only two of many facets that promise to multiply these problems to the sixteenth power each decade. It's not a case of modern man raking the nearest most plausible and utilitarian kind of religion; it is, rather, that he has to develop one quickly with the same effectiveness that he has done his other technology, or he will "progress" himself right out of business, becoming a society without dignity or identity, made up of people who are not persons, who have therefore no conscientious social values, who cannot love. If we do not perish at the muzzles of our own super-cannons, we will evaporate because our brothers do not recognize us.

It may be straining the point overmuch to say that it is a time to "return to" religion, because there's really very little relevant to return to. But what there was back there was something positive, so it might be said that it's time to get serious again. No world will long be able to tolerate the crossed swords of global contact and economic disparity. The artificial exercises that we have to put ourselves through explaining the imbalance of food and fun, forlornness and famine that our instantaneous information keeps rubbing in our faces will eventually destroy those very qualities we want to nourish to stay human. Therefore, what we have to reconsider is our humanity. That's where religion began in the first place.

Now it is time to stop for a moment and look back. We started out investigating the underlying Biblical myths because we are dealing with the problem of the cancerous unhappiness of human depression. We not only found we had to look the earthy, moral, emotional realities squarely in the face, but soon we were caught up in the quickened pulse of a rather hopeful anticipation of the new Man, justifying the saving of Noah. Strange, isn't it, that we who can identify so closely to the despair of a distraught God, knowing perhaps better than most men what it is to be emotionally disillusioned and exhausted, we are the ones who so quickly find ourselves getting into the act of spelling out a new Man? Such is the power and up-to-dateness of the myth. Whether it *happened* somewhere, some ancient time, is no longer of any importance at all. It is happening all the time as a characteristic of human life: destructive despair to tolerance to endurance to hope to covenant. Mayhap, full cycle goes back to despair again, but not quite the same, for life goes on.

So much for the generalities; a new Man is a safe and distant category. But what about me, the lonely estranged exception? Why should I bother with all this big stuff when I hurt so much and don't really care to be dragged in or even want to be healed. Believe me, nothing would be better than to be the dispenser of fixing answers, to give the sure word that here, or somewhere, is to be found the elixir. But we have arrived at the point where recovery from depression depends on a mysterious and completely unmanipulatable arena for decision. The myth has made an outstanding lunge in the direction of man, coming from nowhere and invading his sphere with a story about divine motion that went from negative to positive so that we could live in freedom. In God's act of directing the salvation of Noah is symbolized his timeless respect for what man might be, and for what *I* might be. But having wiped the earth clean of everything else that was wrong, he said to Noah, and to all men, and to me: "Go ahead. I have gone as far as I can go without limiting your freedom. I trust you, I promise never again to lose complete faith. Whatever happens from here is up to you."

This is what God says to any man wherever he is, even if it is a miry pit. The story makes two more points, the down-to-earth realities of what God and man will each be doing from now on. The first point is that Noah, in his drunken disobedience, will go on being a disappointment to God and a liability to society. The second point, signaled by the rainbow, is that God is going to give all men the air space they need without interference to glorify the grandeur or mess in the misery, or both. And, further, God will patiently await, and eternally hope, for the best.

Here is where the crisis comes for the man who has lost his footing and is, as Shakespeare said, "in disgrace with Fortune and men's eyes . . . all alone beweep[ing] my outcast state." Dammit all, anyway! I didn't want some big philosophical fairy tale thrown in my face, I wanted help! But in this case, help only comes in the extended invitation to understand the dimensions of your real freedom, and *you* have to choose the way you will interpret what this means, living with the consequences. But the myth has brought a measure of identity and understanding of your very alienated, bruised withdrawal, and a course of recovery by hoping in the improbable. The rainbow covenant is placed in the sky of every man's heart-horizon as an invitation to the intuition to keep hoping. God, who has much more reason than you do to lapse into cynicism, has decided he never will. Total cynicism at the top level of all creation, then, is out—out forever. It's a promise.

I must acknowledge that this gets to me. I know cynicism and I know hostility and I have been captivated by the luxury of bitterness. But because of this myth, and its later Biblical refinements, I have never been able to sell out completely, or irrevocably. Not that it took determination or fight or inner strength. It was just there, as a given, as the Genesis Assumptions for Living were given to me by a tradition that had been through ten thousand times more grief than I. Hey, fellas, look! I'm dreaming of a new Man! Me!

What held me together in those many situations of terror-filled endurance, when I really would have much preferred to give the whole thing up? How did I ever last through that hour-after-hour, day-after-day longing for the courage to jump off the Golden Gate Bridge? I don't really know, and I have nothing to offer in the way of a "how to." I can only say that once, some unremembered time, maybe twice, I thought I saw a rainbow. And I seem to remember that it helped.

M O T I F

THE IMPOSSIBLE CITY (Gen. 11:1-9)

The introduction to redemptive history is completed in this fifth story, which turns out to be sort of a starting gun for man to become a responsible society. The Tower of Babel appears to suggest the division of mankind into nations and cultures from an original unity, but there is even more meaning to those who give it a closer look.

This myth has been misnamed about a tower. The story really centers about a city, an organized society. "Come, let us build ourselves a city, and a tower with its top in the heavens, and let us make a name for ourselves, lest we be scattered abroad upon the face of the whole earth."

To which the Lord responds with the comment that "nothing that they propose to do will now be impossible for them." Evidently God considers this ability to be an unwanted turn of events, for the next step is a breaking up of the community by making them unintelligible to each other and dispersing them "abroad from there over the face of all the earth."

This is the first of a long and yet endless series of pictures of an ideal society seen in the form of a successful city. Zion, Jerusalem, the Holy City, the Eternal City, the City Foursquare as seen in both Ezekiel and the Apocalypse, Augustine's "City of God," Aquinas' "Heavenly City," Calvin's Geneva, Roger Williams' Providence, and Brigham Young's Salt Lake City, all of them cities, where men live together in interaction in the "realities"—

economics, commerce, politics, law, education, belief. "City" in the profoundest sense of the Greek word *polis* has come to be the word symbolizing the best of what man can be in institutional life, therefore the word describing man at the most ideal fulfillment of collective existence. It describes the symbolic assurance that when men put their best efforts together in a responsible society, the resulting collage is a picture of real man. "Let us make a name for ourselves." Let us discover the Completed Whole of which each of us is a significant but fragmented part.

It was a search for image, identity, confirmation. It was a realization that man is indeed a social animal whose inner resources are stabilized by being in reciprocal contact with his peers, playing as important a part in their lives and welfare as his own struggle for himself. As such, this and any effort toward a responsible society is a parable in amplitude of what goes on inside a man's soul as he tries to put the several parts of complex personality together to "make a name for himself," to find out who he is.

The big stinger about this myth is that it failed. The Bible hasn't even started its narrative about wayward Israel yet, and already we are told that unified societies and cooperative social organization won't work as neatly as they should. Again, one has to take note of the startling realism of this particular family of ancient folktale, as over against most of the rest of antiquity's observations. A terribly oversimplified definition of "existentialism" would be that it is the line of thought more preoccupied with the "is" than the "ought." In this sense, these myths are existential, more interested in depicting what the situation about man really *is* than what fantasy, guilt, or conscience says it should have been. This society was a plain, outright flop.

The importance of the tale is found in the reasons for its failure, and they come through quite clearly. There are two: a presumptuous conclusion that social organization creates a new kind of humanity (a "name" or a new super-human identity) and a loss of communication within.

Concerning the first, it is a paradox that man gets this divine slap on the wrist at first, and then is led through centuries of development of structures, laws, moralities, sensitivities, and sanctions as a way to express God's will. But that, of course, is the whole point. It failed because man was using his very capable intelligent resources to put together a society to put himself on a par with his creator. This is the meaning of the Tower, a place from which man could see the universe and himself from the perspective of God and thereby solve the mystery of his own being and become the controller of his own destiny. It wasn't just that he underestimated the majesty of God; he also underestimated the majesty and meaning of man. He had blasphemously oversimplified himself. You can see the similarity between the city tower and an anthill colony. This ancient-man's answer to his own complex unseen problems was just too simple to work out.

This happens also to be our frequent personal problem. We keep thinking that we have problems or needs that can be solved organizationally, or programmatically, or procedurally. "I don't know what's the matter with me; I just ought to be able to get hold of myself." Angered and frustrated because, whatever we do or try, we don't seem to get it completely under control, we are protesting that there is no panel of switches at our fingertips to reprogram our pains. Just as the Tower of Babel myth is the testimony that man had too small a picture of himself, so are many of our emotional upsets the betrayal of our underappreciation of what it is to be human. It is established at the threshold of the Bible that his book is going to maintain a staggeringly and uncompromisingly high view of man. So, too, hopefully, can it establish to the reader that it is his heritage to have a high and wondering respect for himself.

Depression is the loss, or temporary paralysis, of self-esteem. It is the jumping to an unwarranted conclusion that what we see in the mirror isn't worth striving for, or that it is so balled up that the untangling would cost more in pain than it would justify.

Of course, depression isn't the only result of the loss of the sacred, but whatever damage it wreaks is unnecessary and harmful. Yet, as in the ancient story, we fall into this at the very moment when we think we are thinking big. The folk of this society assumed that they could carry it off, and the text agrees that they could. The point was that what they thought they could do wasn't big enough and was too big all at once. Their error lay in feeling adequate to accomplish too little a goal. The result was disintegration. Is this not also a picture of some of us, one at a time?

The assuring element is the refusal of God to let his precious creature get away with his own downgrading and his scattering of them into more arenas of possibility. I can't help thinking of the many "model families" I have known. Oriented closely around the "American ideal" of close regulation and parental unity, these homes were always a pleasure to visit because there was an atmosphere of pleasantness, and the children would go obediently to their rooms to study when the word was given. Surely, this kind of home would seem to have all the irregularities of modern life under control! One would certainly expect that from these homes would come the healthy leaders of a newly moral society. And so they do—somewhat. But the many, many trips I have had to make back to these same houses, to puzzle through the dilemma of a son in trouble with the police over a stolen car or use of drugs, or a pregnant daughter, or an impending divorce, lead me to feel that there is no such thing as a perfect home. As a matter of fact, I have come to cast a jaundiced eye on the homes that look too good, for fear that they may feel overconfident that they have the situation licked. To add to the mystery, from some of the least promising domestic settings have come leadership of amazing moral dedication. Yes, I know that the statistics generally bear out that better people come from the better regulated homes. The only point being pressed here is that there is neither a magical formula nor a mechanically prefabricated way to conduct family life that will guarantee virtue, wealth, and happiness. God just doesn't let it work out that simply; there's a far greater richness to humanity than that. It was, in fact, the fear that man may become so simplistic and procedurized that made God (or cumulative human insight, or the wisdom of many centuries, or the sagacious appraisal of reality, or whatever) declare the whole city impossible.

Ah, but it is that second reason for failure that brings to a close the introduction to Babel with a wistful brilliance! " 'Come, let us go down, and there confuse their language, that they may not understand one another's speech.' . . . Therefore its name was called Babel, because there the Lord confused the language of all the earth." The community had to disintegrate because its citizens lost communication with each other.

This is probably a way of saying that they failed in their common goals because the goals turned out not really to be that common. When they talked of peace, and harmony, and an organization of society that met their needs, they meant very different things. When it got down to the specifics, where one man was saying "peace" another was translating "defense" while a third was thinking "strong military aggressiveness" and others saw no walls at all. Or that when it came to the acquisition and preparation of food, some saw it to be cooperative and others preferred it "every man for himself."

Even these guesses may be too sophisticated for the primitive experience that brought on the myth. But they are still apropos to the main point. Man does not understand himself, much less understand his neighbor. There is more to meeting real human needs than bows and arrows; the finer nuances of respect, justice, care, and affection are so real that we assume them all too easily. So when any organizational system seems to fill the bill of answering everybody's questions, somebody is certain to rise up and say: "No, no, no. That's not what I meant at all!"

Now that over a half century has passed since the Bolshevik take-over in Russia, it is interesting to examine the original cadre of zealots who brought about the new order, to see if they even understood each other. The testimony is rather clear that they didn't, and the differing points of view had to be disposed of as they came to cross purposes with the leadership junta. In 1937, after but two decades, only 13 percent of the old Bolsheviks survived, with three fourths of the casualties accounted for by purge. In 1957 there were only 5 percent, and now all but one are gone. Why? Did they really defect, become apostate and change their courses traitorously in some midstream? Probably not, as the story of Trotsky clearly reveals. They just had varying concepts of what it meant to be a Communist agent of revolutionary change, with subtle cleavages in doctrine that became amplified as they had the opportunity to be specific. Those who were not at the very top of the heap were circumstantially unfortunate, and probably went to their executions or Siberia or wherever, bewilderedly sincere. It was a genuine but tragic lack of successful communications with a minimum of effort on anybody's part to listen to the other, and a ready resort to accusation as a way of accounting for it. It was probably the same way in Babel, with the whole community turning out to be the victim.

Actually, it is this way everywhere. All units of human life have so many variables and complexities that no one *really* understands or communicates. This applies equally to individuals and societies. Sick societies make no provision for clarifying or understanding or communicating and pay outlandish prices in justice and integrity. Healthy ones find ways of opening channels and traditions of tolerance, and stay healthy only as long as the channels are open. A police state, though it may last a while in time, is a very sick society. I walked the streets of the Soviet Union in the early post-Stalin era. I saw the frightened glances over the shoulder, the masked eyes, the withheld feelings. I found the hidden microphone in my hotel room, and made several Soviet citizens thoroughly miserable (unintentionally) by challenges to open conversation. And over all there hung a feeling of dread and dreariness, of indescribable heart-heaviness, that I didn't fully understand then. Several years later when the blight of emotional depression surrounded me like a cloud, I recognized the same heaviness. It must be hastily added that there have been certain critical occasions in American life since then that have given me the uneasy sensation of limited communication and the beginnings of national sickness.

Remember what has been said earlier about self-deception? Essentially, it means that a person has lost effective communication with himself, that different aspects of his personality are operating without any consideration or allowance for other parts. And in my case, as with so many, the result is a sickness unto death. Recently the governor of a great state was caught in a public misrepresentation. A sensationalistic columnist was merciless in his exposure of the political dishonesty. The governor, known to everyone as a man of high principle but without great wisdom, maintained his action and its cover-up untruth were justified by the circumstances. It appeared to be a case of a man refusing to accept publicly or privately the realization that he had made an ethical and tactical miscalculation. Being the man he is, there is every probability that he believes his own words utterly. If so, he has a problem.

A teen-age boy was known to be a notorious cheater on his schoolwork. Unfortunately, he was gifted with a skillful and argumentative tongue; on the many occasions he was confronted by school authorities for his cribbing, he could come up with the most amazingly plausible explanations. Exasperated, faculty and friends let him get through school. The only one he really fooled was himself, and on many occasions since then, he has lied himself into places his tongue couldn't ease him out of; he simply can't understand why the world treats him so badly. His "do-er" self is out of touch with his "be-er" self and he's sick. The syndrome is at its caricatured best in Scarlett O'Hara, who could pass off any infectious honesty that threatened to bridge her schizophrenia with an "I'll think of that tomorrow."

All of us tend to be little Babels. We start off by thinking that the idea of the existence of God can be handled quite adequately by reason. We go from there to a presumptuous taking over of all controls on living, feeling that if we don't have all the answers right now, they will come in due order. By George, they'd better! Then, to keep the game going, we tend to avoid humility in the pinches, and for some of the least of us, from there to self-deception and the horrors of hell. This myth, this deceptively simple and charming but piercingly profound fable of old, given as one of man's most ancient legends, had us pegged all the time. It makes it rather important for us to review it.

If we're ready for exposure, that is.

RESOLUTION OF THE MOTIFS

These words have been written in the Borough of Manhattan in old New York. This part of the nation's greatest city is built on solid rock, a stony island between a sound and a river. Here the world's tallest building, underground railroads, the United Nations, and millions of people are all quite secure. The rock ledge goes down a thousand feet; we can count on the terrain being around for a while. Of course, it took the creative process several million years to develop the island, but there it is. So, too, have developed over the centuries of human experience a small set of elementary observations that have proven their merit, and on which lives are safely built.

These five basic Assumptions for Living are the meticulously formed bedrock of Western man's living; upon them healthy people and societies do dwell. Even when we are not aware, which may be most of the time, their imprint offers strength, stability, confidence.

Creation! This day-to-day being whose endless monotony can at times seem like water sloshing back and forth in a tub is really purposeful motion, started in calculation and guided in direction. Tomorrow need not be a dull echo of yesterday, but a new step in personhood!

The Fall! Humanity *does* have personalizing options, a dizzying dominion of moral challenge, and the constant invitation to choose the directions of life and love. We may misuse our birthright, but we *never* lose it.

Fratricide! This is a cruel mirror that shows with unwanted accuracy our animalistic viciousness and the senseless consequential pain, yet refuses to state that this robs us of warm, wanting, loving, interacting humanity. It's still there.

The Death of Cynicism! Above the despair and futility that both God and man know only too well is a hope, a covenant, and a promise. Not only will God and all healthy men refuse to resort to complete hopelessness, but both will dream of a coming new Man.

The Impossible City! Man will never completely understand himself, but neither man nor society will be completely disintegrated because of it; life is a constant pilgrimage to making what communication and understanding there is as functional as possible. Instead of being a state of "arrival," life is the adventure of "arriving." The healthy accept it for that.

We didn't start out on this examination with any claims that the myths provide answers to the loneliness of a sick, divided, and despairing personality. We just said that these are good things to know, available stepping-stones to the insights that lead to health.

They just might be.

FOURTH
REFLECTION

Death and Resurrection

1:30 A.M. Sunday morning.

Finally aware that that distant annoying jangle was the telephone, he clumsily groped around the floor by the bed. He seemed to be aware that the interruption was somewhat of a relief to him. Then he remembered as he put the handset to his ear that it had been a horrible night so far, during the two hours of staring in the dark and flip-flopping around on the bed, and the restless shallow sleep. He'd been brooding again.

"Hello?" A crisp, urgent voice spoke quickly, pleadingly. "O.K."—now wide awake—"I'll come right away."

So her time has come. That's good; she's suffered enough. I haven't seen anyone put up a fight like that in years. I don't believe she ever lost her spunk. But these last two months have been pretty hard, watching those eyes sink into those big sockets, that frail little body shriveling up. She's probably only about eighty pounds now, less than half her healthy weight. Well, up and at it!

Clothes fumblingly assembled in the right order, even in the dark. Shave? No time for that. The hospital's forty miles up the freeway; he must get there for the last minute. Down the stairs he tiptoed, picking up the New Testament off the desk in the study, into the cool night, and to the car.

Two blocks from home, a stoplight. Why do they leave those fool things on all night, when there's no traffic? As if to chasten his impatience, a truck came by. The light stayed red for so long he thought it might be stuck.

There's something very unreal about this. Here they call for me to come from the next county to bring them spiritual help in time of death. *Me.* If they knew what I really feel about death, they would be quite upset. I guess a clergyman's appearance at a time like this is completely priestly, symbolic. I don't have to be a sincere, believing, strong, assuring person; I just have to go and repeat the old words. And I suppose that's a help in itself, worth the trip.

Out on the highway he wound up the little Volkswagen to a cool seventy, leaned back, and turned on the radio. It was a pleasant surprise to find a station on at that hour, even more pleasant that it offered classical music all night long. The orchestra had just begun Richard Strauss's capricious "Till Eulenspiegel's Merry Pranks."

"Till Eulenspiegel"? What's that about? Oh, yes. An old German folktale about a young man who just couldn't take anything seriously: life, or work, or love, —or death. He just had to laugh at anything, spring off a practical joke on everybody including those who loved him. He even makes a travesty out of his own funeral.

If there ever really was such a person, he must have been grotesquely pathological. He had to use humor in its worst sense to avoid any kind of direct contact with the world.

But who am I to talk? Here I am, tooling along in the

middle of the night to be with a family who are hurting and grieving down to their shoetops. I'm not hurting. I'm taking the whole thing rather lightly. As a matter of fact, I'm feeling grateful that the whole thing came up to get me out of the house and that damned blue funk I was in.

I sometimes wonder if I really do have any personal compassion for people. I do enjoy a system that needs my outward presence, and I'm glad the old girl is dying. No, it's not a gladness from any real joy from believing in the Christian resurrection. It's a plain old everyday self-centered gladness to have something to do that looks like it might be appreciated.

Preoccupied, he wasn't too careful about his driving. The buoyant music, the hiss of air coming in the vent, the pain within, the sense of unreal detachment—he was in a special world. The little car crested a hill too fast. An oncoming car refused to dim headlights, came on, and on, and on. Coming alert with a jolt, he realized there was a wet film on the windshield, blurring the strong light. Gluing his eyes to the lower right corner of his field of vision, he plunged on.

The approaching car snarled by. At that instant a shape loomed up in the road in front. With a gasp he slammed at the brake pedal. It was a big, old-fashioned home-built house trailer lumbering along in his lane without taillights. Brakes locked, tires clutched at the pavement in screaming desperation. He managed to miss impact narrowly by careening off the shoulder to the right. Reflexes of driving experience brought the foot off the brake, the wheel turned in the direction of the skid. The little car made a double fishtail right and left through the gravel, and a final broadside along a small ditch bank.

Then he was sitting alone in the night drenched in a cloud of heavy dust, watching the oblivious driver pull his awkward mobile home by. The radio continued to blare the story of the playful German neurotic as he waited for the visibility to clear.

Well! I haven't had a scare like that in years! Funny that it should come tonight, of all nights. Funny too that it should be just at the point in the music where Till is taunting the friends who think he is dead!

I was almost a goner there. Odd—I'm not shaking, or mad at that guy. Or even upset. If I had gone, so what? I'm pretty well insured, my family is on its way to self-sufficiency. I'm not afraid to die!

That's not the way to say it. Maybe I wish I were dead. I can't forget those hours of dread that the telephone call, that merciful call, interrupted. Maybe she decided to die tonight to rescue me from living in that mess another hour! Maybe Till passed off in sick humor what I am passing off in looking respectable. Oh, that steel band around my chest!

He realized that he had slowed to forty, and picked it up a bit. After passing the car and trailer, he had the full four-lane road all to himself. As he watched the way his headlight beams stabbed into the darkness, he felt quite insulated from anything, anything at all. Just driving on. He wondered what it would feel like to go on without stopping, drive to the end of the world and drop off. Till Eulenspiegel had upset all the booths at the fair, frightened his beloved girl friend, and was in essence glee-fully shaking his fist in the face of the devil.

Such is the drama of life and death, whatever that is. I wonder, do I know enough about life to have anything to contribute to the subject of death? Have I ever really taken life one fraction as seriously, as responsibly, as she has? It used to exhaust me to talk with her for the names of the people she asked about. It was uncanny

how she seemed to be *aware* that people needed attention, and somehow she arranged to see that they got it.

It wasn't really exhaustion; it was more likely guilt.
I felt bad that I was a pastor and she was an ordinary
layman but that she looked on the whole congregation
much more pastorally than I ever did.

Yes, that's it. It always made me feel uncomfortable
that she was so much more *alive* than I. Ironic, isn't it,
that she's the one who's dying tonight, and I live on.

He knew the turnoff well; after all, he'd been this way two or
three times a week for the last two months. A short off-ramp to
the right, then a left turn into the underpass, and once again an
interminably long traffic light.

Old rapscallion that I am, I do think there is a close
connection between the ability to live and the *freedom*
to love. She never seemed to be burdened with the depressions or blue moods, even in these painful weeks.
They used the word "cheerful," and that does describe
her. There were times when I thought it was put on,
but when I really got to thinking about it, a truly depressed person just can't put anything on.

Was she just blessed with a sunny personality and a
carefree life? Nope. Can't make much of a case for that.
Her quick identification with other people's emotional
twists showed some scars. I'll bet that girl has really had
some problems that would send most women under.
What is the difference between her and the likes of me?
Glandular? Moral? I live in a world that's like a suffocat-
ing box; she seems to be on a wide open plain, looking
at and caring for everybody.

He realized that the light had changed twice over, and with a
dazed lurch raced the throttle and let out the clutch. Three blocks

to the main street, left one block, then five blocks up the hill.
Not another car in sight, not another sound. He paused at the
boulevard stop and looked up at the hospital, sizing up the
approach to the nearly empty parking lot. He glanced at his
watch: 2:35 A.M.

Well, there it is. Heartbreak Hotel. She is in there, and
she's dying, and I'm coming to bring the last rites of the
Holy Church, and I'm deader than she is. And the family
will greet me like the Angel Gabriel himself bringing in
the kingdom with a trumpet blast.

Why the hell do I go through with this? Why can't I
at least feel human, let alone saintly? I really ought to
love them. I wish I could love them. I wish I could love
as genuinely as she does. Or did, whatever it is now. O
God, help me go through this masquerade without hurting anybody.

Sure enough, there was a son-in-law in the parking lot. Nearly
speechless with feeling, they gripped hands and started up the
steps with those masculine leaps of men in a hurry. The nurse at
the desk looked up, jerked her head toward the left, smiled as
they passed.

"You got here just in time, Pastor. She lost consciousness about
nine thirty. Been sinking fast. It's the last few minutes."

Deathbed scenes have a special formality in intimacy. Almost
always the room is darkened, with only a night light in the far
corner. The family stands around the bed, speaking awkwardly,
softly, almost incoherently. There lay the guest of honor, eyes
half opened, pupils rolled up, breathing in shallow, irregular
gurgling gasps, grayish-green around the open lips, one hand half
clutching the coverlet. She was out of it, far too comatose to ever
communicate with this world again.

He moved quickly to the bedside, put one hand on the warm
forehead, bowed his head for prayer.

O.K., God, so what do I say here? May her soul rest in peace? Wherever she's going now, you and she have pretty well taken care of for some time already. You just gave her the kind of start in life that's going to go wherever it's going to go in the best of style, and you don't need any advice from me now. Save her from dying? Nobody in this room wants me to say that, unless it would mean complete recovery. I'm not even sure the family would go for that if it meant months of convalescence. To heck with what they want, I'll just say what I want, and it's not even addressed to you, God, though you can listen in since the family thinks I'm praying.

Good-by, old girl. You're a pretty remarkable person, and I'm glad we were friends, though at a safe distance. Whatever happens to you now, live it up!

The nurse moved up on the other side of the bed, adjusted her stethoscope, listened. The breathing diminished, shallower, less frequent. The room was very quiet, all eyes on the face that was gradually losing its appearance of strain as the muscles relaxed, and the end was coming on in that undignified dignity of a sinking ship.

The breath spasms had been getting farther apart, shorter, quieter. Between each little wheeze was a long, suspenseful silence; each person in the room stood unblinking, silent, unmoving. It had been many, many seconds, perhaps a full minute or so after the last little flutter when each looked at the other questioningly. Nurse nodded, pulled the earplugs out, crossed herself.

"Oh, Mother, Mother, Mother." Sobs.

Almost involuntarily, as though it were another self, he said, "Blessed in the sight of the Lord is the death of his saints." And then, "Surely, goodness and mercy shall follow me all the days of my life and I shall dwell in the house of the Lord forever."

He had heard himself say the words, but wasn't quite sure

whether they came from inside. But like a visitor from above, there descended a long period of silence. Life and death paraded an invisible pageant, reflected in the glistening eyes of the little bedside company. Somebody said softly, "Yes. Yes. Good-by, Mother."

Now the pastoral role came through in what looked like leadership. "Come now, the nurse has things to do here. Let's go into the lounge for a cup of coffee together." Shepherding them with his warm but firm tone, gesturing to the door, following them down the tiled hall to the drab little utility room the nurses had fixed up for such times.

How about that? Not even a prayer at the bedside. They wouldn't have heard it anyway, and it would have been a pious falsity for me. Now we'll get down to a little grief therapy. Gracious! I'd better make it quick; it's almost dawn and today's Sunday. I'll be a walking corpse tomorrow. I mean today. Come to think of it, I'm that already.

Oh, well, relax. This is a very special time for the family, and I'll give them all I've got, whatever it is. Hope it helps.

"You know, Pastor, there's one thing I never heard you preach about. This is the time for you to tell us just what is heaven, what is hell, and are we sure Mother is in heaven?"

He felt quite comfortable with that. Settling the family down at a small low coffee table, he pulled up a leather lounge chair, put his fingers tip-to-tip, leaned back to give his profound and pastoral deliverances.

"Well, you see, when the Holy Scriptures use these words, they're talking about conditions, not places. Simply put, heaven is the condition of knowing and being in fellowship with God, and hell is the condition of being separated from God, or from honest interaction with the reason for being."

They all looked properly stunned.

"Now then, if there's anyone I ever knew who lived a life in fellowship with God, it's your mother. And at this very minute, it is my very deep faith that that kind of living relationship cannot be destroyed by organic death."

"Do you mean to say that if we live our lives out of fellowship with God we wind up in hell? Are you *sure* that Mother is free from hell?"

So hell is being seperated from God. Just hearing my own voice prattle off that old stock saying rocks me. It must be the hour; I'm very drowsy. If anything describes the way I feel, it is separation from. . . . But, *man,* those old pictures of burning and torture and eternal hopelessness seem awfully familiar to me. Great God! Am I to be a nonperson clear into eternity?

"I'm quite sure. Your mother was so very much alive when it came to expressing the compassion of Christ toward *everybody,* that she's thinking more of us and others right now than she is of herself."

Whew!

But somehow he knew he was hitting pay dirt, at least for himself.

The widower spoke, slowly, for the first time. "Yes. She had her faults. Sometimes I'd get pretty mad at her. But, God bless her . . ." The voice trailed off and all six people stared at the floor for forty-five seconds. "She lived for us. And when she hurt, she hurt for us. She had developed a special attitude I could never understand. It was like no matter how picky we were, she was on our side. You couldn't ever get her down."

A daughter smiled over her knotted handkerchief, "And now she's on the side of the angels."

"No," said the parson, "She's still on our side."

"Why aren't there more like her?" the other daughter said. "And why aren't there more like you, Pastor?"

God, what a jolt. I'm not like that. I brood, I think only of myself. I'm in a first-class depression right now that's entirely my own selfish fault, and I can't crawl out of it for all the tea in China. These people are hungrily begging me to let down my clerical reserve and just be a compassionate human being with them, and I can't. *I can't!* That's what hell is, not to be able to love, or to care, or to be emotionally involved. I just don't care that much, and I'll be so glad to get out of here, to be on that peaceful stretch of road home.

"I suppose," he was fabricating an appropriately dignified answer fast, "we should give thanks that there are such people at all. It gives us all hope to keep on trying."

What a sheer, unadulterated, crass piece of tripe, and from my own lips at that! Who the hell's trying? I'm not, and I'm getting more withdrawn as the conversation goes on. O Lord, have mercy!

"That's just about the most beautiful thing I've ever heard." A very assured look had come over her face. "I don't think I'll ever forget the completely lovely look on your face as you said that."

Oh, God!

The widower again. "You know, Preacher, I guess you'll never in your life be able to know what strength you brought into our lives. As you know, she and I came out of a pretty old-fashioned conservative background, and long after we were married we just couldn't even go to church because we were so fouled up with the literal heaven with the streets of gold and the heavenly city and all that. Your sermons, and your Bible study classes, and your own life made heaven a thousand times bigger and more real and more here on earth. I think she's already been in heaven for some time, but it was even more so since we were lucky enough to come under your ministry." His clear, calm eyes never once relinquished their commanding, heartfelt look with the pastor's.

I feel sick. Shall I run for the can, or just walk out, or sit here and take it? I didn't bring a single solitary whit of anything to these two. They had it all on board when we first met, and even then, four years ago, I was the threatened inferior. They never knew it, or if they did, they never showed it. There's a burning pain in my stomach and a pounding in my chest that I can't tolerate another minute. O Merciful God, what shall I do?

To his relief, the son-in-law spoke. "If hell isn't a place to go for punishment, just what is it? Why do we still talk about it?"
Good. Now we're off my back and I can return to my canned lecture, mused the cleric. "As I said, hell is separation, trying to make the pieces of life fit together without the redeeming love of God."
"Sounds pretty lonely."
"Yes, I imagine it is."

I know damned well it is. And what makes it hell is that I have nobody to blame but myself.
Yes, that's it!
Hell is the loneliness of being in a fix that nobody else shares, nobody understands.

"Then she is certainly not in hell," the other daughter whispered. "She was never lonely. I'd run over to the house when

Daddy had been away on a trip for several days, and she'd either be singing at her work or have the house stacked with company."

"I'll bet you," a son-in-law took a long drag on his cigarette, "that she's already organizing a committee in heaven to make rescuing visits to hell." Laughter.

"In that case," said the older man, "she ought to be turning up in this town soon. There are lots of people here," it seemed that he turned for an overlong glance at the minister, "who live in hell every day."

Omigosh. Does he know? Have I been found out? I may not care enough to love, but I sure have been putting up a ferociously good act to protect my family.

"But"—clerical composure slowly returned as the blush receded—"she's already pulled more people out of hell by her loving concern than we'll ever know about. I think she'll probably be reassigned to some other field." More laughter. The atmosphere was relaxing.

They all made a refill visit to the coffee dispensing machine in the corner, stretched, looked out of the window, wandered slowly back and sat down in a different arrangement.

"Pastor"—the widower again—"I know that before we leave this room, you're going to ask us to pray together. Why? Is it going to make any difference for her?"

Off guard again. He had already wondered if the healthy levity and grief-resolving turn of the conversation might be destroyed by a call to prayer, bring on a morbidity that would be unnecessary here. "Well, of course, she's better off than we are. So I guess our prayer would be one of glad thanksgiving that God fulfills his promises."

Except for me.

I can't feel that God's promises really mean that much to me. I remember when my own parent died, and I was there as I am here. Prayer was the farthest thing from my mind that night, just gratitude that the ordeal was over. If I had really been sensitive to what these good folk need, I would have been harping on the thanksgiving theme long before this. But I was so all-fired anxious to play the part that I never really thought of them.

Just myself.

"I knew you'd say that. You always come up with the sparkling thing in life, just as you do in your sermons."

"But let's not pray yet," the quieter daughter protested, "because that may mean we have to go home. I don't want to cut off this conversation. I just know that when I get to the house I'll come all apart and cry without stopping for days. I need more of this."

He stole a secret look at his watch. 3:26 A.M.

She went on. "Tell us what you think about Mother and the resurrection. Will we see her again?"

Again a moment of professional confidence. Here, too, out of the necessities of many scenes like this, he had a condensed and carefully ambiguous line put to memory about the eternal love of God and the certainty of the resurrection. But suddenly, as he looked at the five waiting faces, the quiet but disturbed eyes, he felt he had nothing to say.

"Well, to be quite honest—"

A distracting thought ricocheted off the other daughter's mind, bringing a providential interruption. "Oh, I haven't prepared myself for this at all. What are we going to tell the children? Are they old enough to understand death? Will they ever see their grandmother again?"

What a temptation to launch into the old fairly tales this is. I could tell her that she could tell her children that when they die they'll all be together somewhere. I don't really believe that, and right now I'm too tired to

lie, too tired to dish out stuff just for the effect. Why not
level with these people at this very crucial minute in
their lives?

Of course, they might not be emotionally prepared for
it. But then again, this is no time to feed them outright
balderdash.

That's one advantage of living in hell as I do. In not
caring, I might offhand do something worthwhile that I
wouldn't have the nerve to do otherwise.

"No, don't tell them they'll see her again." The expected gasp,
the chill. "Resurrection is a total mystery that we ought not to
fool with in our earthbound fantasies. I don't know what it is,
and I'm not sure I believe it in the traditional way." He certainly
couldn't have complained that his audience wasn't listening.

"You mean you think she's gone forever?"

"Yes. Gone. At least, the person we knew. Never to live again.
Completely final."

"Then the Christian teaching of the resurrection is a lie?"

"Not at all. It's just that we have read into the resurrection an
insistence that life will continue as we know it and like it and
want it to stay. And that's probably pretty close to blasphemy."

"But what do we celebrate on Easter?"

"Something we couldn't possibly understand. Some phenome-
nally majestic development about truth conquering falsehood,
good triumphing over evil, and life crowned as superior to death."

Oops, that sounds like homiletic gobbledygook. But
I've opened this can of worms, and I just can't leave it
there, for their sake.

"Pastor, let me ask you a very personal question."

I'm so damned sick and tired of wearing a mask that
I'll just answer this question straight, and let the chips

fall where they may. What does it matter? I'm in hell already, anyway.

"Do you look forward, yourself, to life after death?"

"No."

"Oh, I can't accept that!" She wasn't waiting to get home. She was crying now, hysterically.

"I thought you came here to help us." The man's eyes had the beginnings of anger, or maybe it was fear.

"I didn't say I disbelieved the resurrection." Instead of getting louder and defensive, as he thought he might, he was quieter, more relaxed. "I just said it would be a misuse of that belief to talk about personal reunion in heaven, or even that she is still the one we knew."

"Then for God's sake, what *do* you believe?" The widower had paced to the far end of the room.

Now there's a good question. What do I believe? Can I tell them that I don't even want to live any more than I have to? Can I tell them that I have made such an irresponsible mess of my life and others whom I love that I would greet total nonexistence gladly? Can I tell them that from the perspective of hell—lonely, grinding, self-despising, degrading hell, death would be a friend? What do I believe?

Funny thing. Bad as I feel, I do believe *something,* whatever it is. It may not be what I want to believe, but it's there.

I guess I've been so wrapped up in my own inward-turned problems, and used the professional shibboleths for so long, that I've never honestly talked this over with myself.

That's the trouble with this church business. There are so many canned answers to the big propositions of life that you can use as a substitute for really dealing with yourself. Well, there's nothing to do now but to turn on the words and listen to myself talk. It will be as much a surprise to me as it will be to them.

"I believe that whatever happened after the crucifixion"—long pause—"and it *was* something so all-consuming important to the apostles that it became the central story of their faith, was a gift from God. It was a community discovery that no defeat is final. Or, you might say, a life lived in awareness that there is a will of God that can never be totally snuffed out. It may appear to be destroyed, but it will reappear in a new form."

The other son-in-law snorted. "You know, I think she'd be happy with that. She and I had a little talk once, ten years or more ago. I don't remember much of it, but I was pretty amazed. For some reason, she got off on the subject of death."

"You never told me about it." His wife sounded childish and petulant.

"No. I didn't really know how. Anyway, the upshot of it was that she wasn't out to win Brownie points by doing good. She really didn't care about going to heaven."

"What are you saying?" More automatic than horrified.

"I'm saying that she lived in the here and now, and wasn't worried about the future. She was—well, I guess the word is— secure."

"Is that what *you* mean, Pastor?" the sobbing daughter.

"Ye-e-es. And more."

"But how about you? Don't you want to feel that when you die there's something more in store?"

"Frankly"—the words began to avalanche before the minister could think—"I don't give a damn. I'm called to live as a responsible human, and all I want to do is to get that monkey off my back in some way resembling the way God wants it. I don't want any reward, and I don't want any more responsibilities. After that, I don't care!"

The stream had started, and couldn't be stopped.

"I've tried to avoid that responsibility," he went on forcefully, almost hostilely, "and believe me, it's a hell of a life. I've just got to be honest with you. I don't even think of God when I'm down. I don't think of others. I think only of myself. And it's hell, and I'm just fed up pretending."

Long silence. Nervous shuffling of feet, changing positions, firing up of cigarettes, throat-clearing. So he went on.

"As far as I'm concerned, this whole schmier of living is centered around the ability to relate to people in an honest, constructive way. When you're so completely crippled and sick inside that you can't see your brother, you're already dead. You're already being consumed by fires of hell."

He stood abruptly, jammed his hands into his pants pockets. "I just don't want to go on that way."

"But Mother was never that way. She wasn't like that!" Half shriek, half whimper from the younger daughter.

Her father stood up, full length, stared at the clock on the wall (4:04 A.M.). He flicked the ash off his smoke onto the linoleum, turned his cupped hand so he could look at the lighted end.

Then he spoke. "Yes, she was. Once."

No, no, no. You didn't understand what I said. She could never have known this trapped selfish inwardness, this kind of terror I have brought on myself. She was free from that curse. She loved.

Father went on. "You girls don't remember your early life too clearly, thank God. There was a stretch of two and a half years when your mother was in and out of a mental hospital three times. I had never heard anyone talk like that again until just now." Turning his gaze, "Pastor, you've got the same problem."

Can't hide now. Don't want to. But she certainly couldn't have been that sick. In a hospital? Oh, good God!

"Daddy! Don't say that! He came out in the middle of the night to help us, and I'm glad he came."

"Yes," said the older man, "I'm glad he came, too. In fact, you will never know how glad I am. Maybe we can all be really truthful at last, for her sake. I had to stand by in those years that she suffered those depressions. It was really much worse then than these last two months have been, by far."

He reached over to the ashtray and blankly tapped the cigarette. "And when she lost hope, believe me, I lost hope, too. I think we both died then."

"Why, yes!" The older daughter was probing back in her memory. "I think I *do* remember that. All I can recall is that when she was home she stayed in her room and you wouldn't let us in. I thought she had some dreadful bug that you didn't want us to catch."

"She was either drugged or in tears. If you had gone in, she would have gone into screaming hysterics or ignored you completely."

A husband asked, "How did she get that way?"

"I don't know. The doctors called it anxiety neurosis. She was too young for menopause. Of course she was worried about her step-father, who was an alcoholic, and that sister of hers who couldn't stay married to the same man for a year straight. And, too, we were having money and marital problems. But to be truthful, she had always been a worrywart and a complainer."

"Mother—"

"Until then, that is. She has been a very different person since she came out of it, and it's the new Mother you know."

I wonder if he even knows what he's talking about. It can't be that she was as far gone as I think I am. She just *couldn't* have been that different from the happy woman I knew. He must be handing out this line of bosh as a way of rescuing my dignity.

"Oh, this is terrible, terrible"—the younger daughter again dissolving. "I wish this whole thing hadn't come up. We're being disrespectful to Mother's memory. You shouldn't have said those things, Daddy. They're wrong!"

"Go ahead," said her father, "cry it out. You're a lot like your mother—used to be. She cried a lot, too."

"Daddy, stop it!" More sobs. "You're cruel. You're teasing me. You know that Mother was the most cheerful, selfless, happy person in our house. Now quit it!"

"As a matter of fact, she wasn't all that good. She was just a damn fine woman who knew what was going on and respected people."

There's a phrase that hits home. She "knew what was going on and respected people." By golly, that's a definition worth remembering!

"DADDY!" She jumped to her feet and ran for the women's restroom, shouting as she left the room: "Unfaithful!"

"Yes," he nodded slowly. "That, too."

The pastor found he was quivering inside. Almost afraid to speak lest it become obvious, he managed to get out, "There must have been a spectacular healing, then."

Father sat down, stretched his long legs out in front, heels cornered on the floor, toes up. "Yes, I guess spectacular is the word, looking back on it. It was more of a miracle to me than the raising of Lazarus must have been to Mary and Martha."

He's talking my language again. He's likening this oblivion to death. It *is* death. Only worse. I long to be alive, and am afraid to live, so I crouch in the shadows and hurt.

Yes, I think I can see it now. There were some phrases she used when we were talking about that doctor's wife

who committed suicide, like she'd been down that road. It didn't hit me then, I just thought she was a very wise woman. But now I see there was more depth to her than any of us suspected.

So. She returned from the tomb!

Father was still talking. "She and I used to discuss it over and over. I kept saying that she could pull herself out of it if she only tried, and she'd just put her head in her hands and moan, 'I can't, I can't.' I didn't know what she was going through, and there were times when I was pretty disgusted with her."

Daughter returned from the washroom, tiptoed in behind her father, sat down slowly, silently, her eyes wide, tear-stained, listening.

"The thing that griped me most was the way she just shut the rest of us out of her life, like she didn't love us anymore, or really care—"

Oh, yes. Oh, God, yes.

"So we went to the doctor, and he sent us to a psychiatrist, and she went to him three times a week, and seemed to pick up a bit. But she had her black days, or weeks. In three cases it stretched out to months, and so she had to go away.

"I think her recovery started once when she was at the hospital. I went to see her on a Sunday afternoon. Her wardmates had been talking about death, and she was pretty upset. She asked me if I was afraid to die, and I said I hadn't thought much about it, but it wasn't a very pleasant thought. So I asked her the same question, and darned if her answer wasn't word for word the same one you just gave, Pastor. It was then that I knew there was a definite connection between her condition and death, and that she had actually tasted of the real hopelessness of death. And I felt that it was more than just a recovery from some disease that she needed, but a calling back from the dead."

Now how can this man be so wise? How can anybody outside this little lonely cell I've been in know so much about it?

Yes, yes! Not a recovery, but a resurrection! I don't know how she did it, but I am hearing for the first time in my life that it has been done. Tell me, tell me!

"Please," said the pastor hoarsely, then clearing his dry throat, "please tell me—us."

The nurse interrupted, "The men from the mortuary are here," gesturing to two men standing in the hall, "and we need your signature on these release papers."

The half hour of arrangements was difficult, distracting. Afterward they were all standing by the back door of the black panel truck that now held the blanket-covered body. The little company, the six of them, watched mutely as the little van started slowly down the sloping driveway, its red stoplights flashing brightly at the stop sign.

The time: 4:59 A.M. They went back into the hospital lounge to get their coats, and as with a signal, all sat with that uneasy perch that says, "Now what?"

He was very anxious to get back to the subject, but it was obvious that the others were very, very weary. Still, he couldn't help asking. "You say that she started to get better at that talk in the hospital?"

Sighing, smoothing out the coat on his lap, the widower looked out of the window as if to find the little truck. "Not at. After. No, I don't know how she did it. It may have been the medical treatment, or it may have been religion. It was about three weeks after she came home that we started going to church, and two or three years after that that she became a Christian. Whatever happened, it was very mysterious to me. It was way deep down inside her. It's a very baffling experience to see a person come to life. You're just a spectator, nothing else. There wasn't a single thing I did to help—just watch. It came from inside her."

"But what *did* happen? What did she do?" The minister was impatient, almost rudely insistent.

"I don't know. I honestly don't know. I guess I can only say that she began to notice the rest of us more. It wasn't that we hadn't mattered to her, but it just seemed that her own ideas and fears and lies had mattered more to her before. Then, somehow, they just shifted, and people came through to her, and her inner pains didn't make that much difference. No, I don't know.

"But you," turning with a warm smile to his minister, "you need to know, and I sure hope you find out, someday."

Older daughter closed her eyes, breathed a deep sigh. "I'm so tired. I don't see how I'll make it home. But I hate to go home. I'll just cry."

Her husband turned to the cleric. "I guess it's about time for that prayer now."

"Yes—yes, I suppose it is." They all rose, instinctively joined hands. Again the trained professionalism almost took over as he reviewed the several memorized classical prayers, but somehow the words wouldn't come out. They stood there in silence. Then he said, "Let's just pray for each other."

Afterward nobody could quite remember what took place in that close circle. Maybe somebody prayed; he was sure he didn't, at least out loud. But they all knew it was prayer, and they all had tears.

Wordlessly, they moved out the door and to the parking lot. As he walked over to his car, he was aware that the one among them who would go home to an empty house was walking with him.

"Pastor," so low as almost to be a whisper, "I don't know any more sacred tribute to her than the real straightforwardness and honesty you shared with us tonight. Whether we understand the resurrection at all or not, it *is,* you know. She knew it, and I believe to my toes that she is a part of it now. You helped me tonight. She prayed for you more than for anyone, you know. Good night. And thanks."

Dazed, he sat in the little car fumbling for his keys. It was dark, very dark, and he was very bewildered.

So she knew about me, all the time. They say it takes one to know one.

And she went to her death praying for me. What a story! I came to minister, and gave nothing, but was ministered unto.

That'll throw me into a darker tizzy for days.

O merciful God!

When he turned the key, both the engine and the transistor car radio jumped into life. Same program, still on, with classical music. Now it was the ascending phrases of Wagner's "Procession of the Pilgrims" from *Tannhäuser*. He'd driven almost a block before he thought to put his headlights on. It was fortunate there was next to no traffic; he wasn't seeing much of the road.

I don't think I want to go home. It'll just be the start of another bad day. I don't even remember the sermon several hundred people are going to hear tomorrow—today.

What did he say? She knew what was going on and respected people. Ever since I've had this damnable anxiety I just haven't been with it.

I *know* that I care, or that I *can* care about others. There's a great deal of genuine life around me that I can respect and want to relate to. But they just seem to glide by like ghosts.

But they're still there. So it isn't the world that's sick, it's me. Maybe, since I haven't troubled myself to know what's going on in their lives, it would help to identify with them more.

I'd like to know what my poor wife thinks is going on. Every time I try to level with her, I get to feeling guilty because it hurts her so much. No wonder she feels rejected, estranged, or as she calls it, unloved. It depresses me to think what she's put up with. Sometimes it's easier to shut the door on her and not even think about it. I *do* care about her. I really do respect her.

Then there are those close friends I've shut out. Too proud to tell them. How about my oldest friend, who really needed me last month? I'm ashamed to think that I was so bound up in my groanings that I still don't know how he handled it.

Guess I'll just screw up my determination and turn outward. Have to. No other way.

The orchestra was proclaiming in solid major brass the triumphant hope of the pilgrims. To his left, the east, the sky was getting light. 5:45 A.M. The sun was giving notice that it would soon arrive.

"Now on the first day of the week, while it was still dark . . ."

The big things that happen to a person, like birth, death . . . and resurrection, aren't his doing. They're gifts, from some mysterious powerful source. I've been trying to raise myself.

He was driving too fast again, he realized. The little car could be tricky in a stiff side wind. Getting a new grip on the wheel, he shifted in the little bucket seat and tightened his seat belt.

So we prayed. Or didn't pray. Did it seem to be prayer to me? Something did happen to me. Like the referee declaring that it was the end of the round and we could go to our corners. Or was it the end of the fight?

I'm tired. Very, very tired. I could sleep now, though I won't have the time. It's refreshing and peaceful to drive this time of morning. Of course my real weariness isn't from the hour, but from fighting this unending internal battle. This conflict.

Jacob fought all night. Didn't he wrestle with "a man" until the breaking of day?

That poor guy was in conflict with himself, all right. His conscience was bothering him about the coming meeting with the brother he cheated.

The brother he *deceived*. Not just that night, but twenty years of putting off the day of reckoning. Oh, the poor man! Pretending to be a righteous man, running from the truth, cheating his father-in-law. That must have been some night!

Deceiving your brother is like deceiving yourself. I wonder if Jacob knew what he was doing.

Twenty years!

O God, O God, O God! Rescue me! Force the truth on me. Make me face my true self. Make me come to my senses. Make me a living person. Let me love. Let me forget myself and get back into the stream of life! O merciful God! You *do* know what all this is. You *do*. Don't leave me alone. I'm afraid. I hurt.

Now he *was* trembling. And he was sick, physically nauseated. And weeping. He pulled off on the shoulder and folded his arms on the steering wheel. Wagner's pilgrims returned from Rome to the rolling cascades of strong affirmative chords and rolling tympani. He turned off the radio, switched off the engine.

There was just enough light for him to see, thirty yards ahead and on the far side of the highway, his own skid marks of a few hours ago. A long, black double stripe that curved across the lane and into the soft dirt shoulder where it became a hook-shaped trench. He might have died there, this very night.

He remembered that at the time, he had actually welcomed the thought of death. Now, he stared at the ugly slash on the pavement, wondering.

A truck snarled by. Its slipstream slapped the little car and rocked it once, sharply. Then its diesel roar diminished as it went on. And on. And down. Then silence. He was alone, all alone.

But not *really* alone. Not panicky. No more quivering. Breathing easily, deeply, peacefully.

Now, how did that story of Jacob and the angel go? Something about getting hurt in the hollow of his thigh, but he kept on fighting. And then when morning came, he was still at it, so the man or angel or whatever it was blessed him. And he gave the place some kind of Hebrew name because he had seen God face-to-face, and lived through it.

Lived through it! It says he had a limp the rest of his life, *but he did come back to life.*

So it is. I've been hurt. Wounded. By my own morbid bungling. I know I'll limp for the rest of my life.

But, somehow, I feel like walking.

He lifted his head. The sky was a majestic tower of gold, reflected by every moist leaf and rock. A new day had started, in that hushed fresh expectancy. A distant car horn sounded like a trumpet.

"If I take the wings of the morning and dwell in the uttermost parts of the sea, even there thy hand . . ."

Much to do today. A beautiful day.

"Thou art there."

So here I am, starting the day as if I belonged here. I think I really do.

He started the car, pausing before shifting into gear for another long, relaxed, appreciative look at the brightening east.

Morning. The first day of the week.